My dear friend, my brother, Lionel Mayell, whose hospitality and generous spirit has meant many happy and precious hours of sweet fellowship. How God has used you in our lives. Both Ruth and I send our love.

—Billy Graham
Founder, Billy Graham Evangelistic Association

In *5'2" Giant*, Rita Mayell traces the handprint of a loving heavenly Father who relentlessly pursues a relationship with us, as told through the life of her father. She writes about the conflict and struggle between a man's dream of success and doing the will of a heavenly Father who has a plan and purpose for those who obediently submit to the will of God. From Lionel's rejection by his own family, to becoming the Father of the Condominium, to having an encounter with God who forever changed his life and the world around him, readers will clearly see that obeying Jesus Christ brings satisfaction beyond anything the world can offer. *5'2" Giant* is a story that will thrill the soul and connect the reader to God's truth: "I can do all things through Christ who strengthens me" (Philippians 4:13).

—Franklin Graham
President & CEO, Samaritan's Purse
Billy Graham Evangelistic Association

My father, Dr. Bob Pierce, considered Lionel Mayell "a friend who stood through thick and thin." During the foundational days of World Vision and later Samaritan's Purse, Lionel gave generously of his financial resources to see God's vision fulfilled. He was also a man who knew what it meant to be a faithful friend and godly counselor. To quote my father at Lionel's 80th birthday celebration, "I could count on Lionel Mayell. ... He gave his financial resources and his time, no matter the hour, and was always willing to help. But most importantly, he listened and never judged. I trust him with my very life." I believe that the world needs more men like Lionel Mayell, and I pray that this book will inspire a new generation to follow his example of generous giving to the work of God in this hurting world!

—Marilee Pierce Dunker
Author of Man of Vision *and daughter of Dr. Bob Pierce,*
founder of World Vision and Samaritan's Purse

Lionel Mayell was an incredible person and a powerful, world-changing dynamo (he'd have been seven feet tall if he weren't wound so tight!). He made up for his small stature by having an oversized heart for God and others.

—Larry W. Poland, Ph.D.
Founder and Chairman Emeritus, Mastermedia International

Lionel Mayell's life story reveals powerful evidence of an ordinary man who encountered God and became extraordinary. He was extraordinary in his vision, his passion for Jesus, his wisdom, and his belief that with God all things are possible. When he joined CRU at age 69, his unstoppable energy and contagious can-do spirit ignited a passion for Christ in everyone he met.

—*Dr. Steve Douglass*
President, Campus Crusade for Christ International/Cru

I loved Lionel Mayell and his family, and was delighted to read Rita's words that pulled back the curtain to gain an intimate look at his life. It was a joy to see what God was doing, through Lionel, to impact Christianity in the world and the lives of Billy Graham and Bill Bright, to name only two. This book brought tears of gratefulness, awe at what God did, smiles, and laughter. You will fall in love with Lionel, his Lord, his life, his faith, and his ripple-effect impact on the world.

—*Ney Bailey*
Author, Faith Is Not a Feeling
Campus Crusade for Christ/Cru

Ritalynn, what memories you evoke from my heart when I hear your name, "Mayell." I recall your dear father and our wonderful days in your home with my late wife Billie. (That goes back to 1949). Your father meant so much to me, as did the whole family, as you know what evenings of delight the team at the Canvas Cathedral had in your home. I remember, so well, your dear dad driving and turning around in the seat to look at Billie and me in the back seat! I grabbed his head, pointed it forward, and said, "Lionel, keep lookin' straight ahead. You're driving us crazy here!" With joy, we faced the challenges and ministry at the Canvas Cathedral. We even had a radio program in your home with Billy Graham as the emcee introducing members of the team. Each gave a little segment on the broadcast. Mr. Graham was young in those days, as I was, and we all got a roaring laugh out of it! This meant so much to us in our personal fellowship and growth with each other. We don't know what we would have done without the loving support and encouragement from your dear, dear father and mother.

—*Cliff Barrows*
Music and Program Director, Billy Graham Evangelistic Association

Your father was more than a co-laborer; he was my dearest friend and confidante. From the early years, I knew your dad when he was in the toy business and I in the confection business. He saw the dream and calling of God on my life and encouraged me with words backed with the first check to start Campus Crusade for Christ. Years later he joined the staff of Campus Crusade for Christ and, in the years when I needed the wisdom and support of a godly man, God sent Lionel Mayell. I could always count on Lionel to support and encourage me. Besides my precious Vonette, your dad was the one with whom I could share my heart. Your dad would listen, give me wisdom and Scripture, and stand by my side. He had the courage to set me straight when I needed it. He was a man of God and integrity, and I will greatly miss him but his precious spirit will remain.

—*Bill Bright*
Founder, Campus Crusade for Christ International/Cru

Lionel Mayell took me in out of the cold and taught me how to walk in the Spirit and how to share and grow. Lionel chipped away at this rough, tough diamond. He took me with him everywhere. He taught me how to pray, testify, and study the Bible. He handed down his ministry to me as a father to his son. He is my "little giant" and to me my big brother.

—*Colonel Heath Bottomly, USAF Retired*
Air Force Bald Eagle of Takhli;
Former Secretary to the Joint Chiefs of Staff at Pentagon;
Holder of Legion of Merit, Distinguished Flying Cross

Through the many years at Youth for Christ, Lionel Mayell was our spark-plug. He kept us all going. Through the dips and valleys, he was always first to say, "Come on, fellas. It will work." That was Lionel Mayell. Time and time again, he not only took us out for a meal but gave sacrificially. He gave when he did not have it to give. He gave when he had it. He gave more than most men consider. He was an example to me as young man, and I'll never forget him. I love his memory and cherish the knowledge that I will see him again.

—*Roy McKeown*
Executive Director, Youth for Christ Greater Los Angeles;
President, World Opportunities International

Of all the men whose lives have, in my judgment, contributed more to the world than they have taken out, the name of Lionel Mayell stands supreme. To those of us who knew him, the mention of his name brings immediate thoughts of generosity and unselfish, undemanding, sacrificial love. I first met Lionel Mayell before I was Christian. I accepted Christ, and Lionel stayed like glue with me, loving me for over two years. He invited me to live in his home. His interest in me, a Hells Angel, both before and after I received Christ was clearly the reason I invited Jesus into my life. I was lonely; he met that need. I was afraid; he met that need. I was discouraged; he met that need. No matter what seemed to be troubling me, Lionel took the necessary time to help me. I had two felony counts, and Lionel stayed with me in the two-year process, writing a letter of commendation to the judge. Lionel did whatever was necessary to help me conquer every situation from my past. He poured the Word of God into me and became a father to me.

Of course, I believe that Christ was the One who conquered my problems, but too often we forget that God uses men. In my life, God used Lionel.

—Rick Carreno
Former Hells Angel;
Founder, Rick Carreno Evangelistic Association

Mrs. Johnson and I join thousands of friends everywhere in paying our respects to a great man of God. The enormity of the contribution that has been made by Lionel Mayell and his beloved wife, Dorothy, to the church of Jesus Christ and to the work of the Gospel will never be fully known till we get the other side.

—Dr. and Mrs. Torrey Johnson
Founder, Youth for Christ

In looking back over our association through the years, I am grateful to the Lord that he put it into your heart to actively seek the salvation and spiritual welfare for the fellows at the McKinley Home for Boys, of whom I was one. You were, to several of us, like a spiritual father at that time and through our college years. And your interest in and prayers for us continued beyond that time as well. Thanks for your loving concern, counsel, and financial support that made our dreams come true. You sent me to college and no one knew.

—Leo and Marlene Skinner
McKinley Children's Center, San Dimas, California

Your ideas have always been young. Your approach has been positive. Your spirit has been wholesome and contagious.

—T. W. Wilson
Executive Assistant to Billy Graham

How does one describe in words, a lifetime friend such as Lionel Mayell? He embodies the very essence of "friendship." He encouraged my vision for Wycliffe, gave financially, and introduced me to people who would encourage us in those formative years. He believed, stood by our side. I respect, honor, and love him. The world honors so many of us: Billy Graham, Bill Bright, Bob Pierce, but none of us would be where we are if it had not been for this man who fanned the flame of vision and gave encouragement, never wanting anything for himself but to honor the Lord Jesus Christ.

—Cameron Townsend
Founder, Wycliffe Bible Translators, JAARS

A man whose one sole desire was to sincerely know God and make Him known. I cannot describe what Lionel Mayell has meant to me personally and what his encouragement and support have done for Navigators worldwide.

—*Dawson Trotman*
Founder, The Navigators

Lionel Mayell visited me in jail and in prison. He did not see me for what I had done but who I could become in Christ. His love for me led me to the Lord Jesus Christ. He demonstrated the love of Jesus, His forgiveness and grace. Lionel Mayell was faithful to encourage me, visit, and write long letters mentoring me in my faith. He became a "father" to me.

—*Dennis Whitney*
Death Row Inmate, Raiford Prison

Your friendship and dedication to the cause of Christ have been a source of rich inspiration through the years. More than anyone I know, your life has been a classic fulfillment of the Mosaic promise, "As thy days, so shall thy strength be (Deuteronomy 33:25)."

—*Dick Ross*
Producer/Director, World Wide Pictures;
President, Billy Graham Evangelistic Film Ministry

Suzy and I have known Lionel and Dorothy for decades. Not once have I ever seen this man moved off course in his faith or vision for the Lord Jesus Christ. If it weren't for their friendship, love, and encouragement, I can honestly say we would not be where we are today.

—*Suzy and Stuart Hamblin*
First Singing Cowboy, Radio Personality, and Songwriter

What can I say about Lionel Mayell other than he embodies the word *friend*. I have never seen a man so quick to help another without any desire to have credit. I quote D. L. Moody, "The world has yet to see what God will do with and for and through and in and by the man who is fully and wholly consecrated to him. I will try to be that man." Lionel Mayell met these qualifications.

—*Cy Nelson*
President, Gospel Light Publications

5'2"

GIANT

BUILDER OF DREAMS

ONE ORDINARY MAN WHO CHANGED THE WORLD

RITA MAYELL

DEDICATION

I dedicate this book to the "giant" I write about and in honor of the One he taught me to follow, the Lord Jesus Christ. My father was small in size, yet with his sincere heart and compassion for others, thinking more highly of others than himself, he has shaped my life more than any other person in this world. His love for Jesus and the simplicity of his belief that with God all things are possible is the core foundation on which my life rests.

However, I could not dedicate this book without acknowledging my mother. My parents were a team, partners, lovers, and best friends, and they personified unity in marriage as one.

Mother and Daddy, today you are a part of the large "cloud of witnesses" cheering me onward. You must revel in the fact that your prodigal daughter finally caught what you spent a lifetime living: God loves me! Yes, He does! He is always for me, and now I look back and see His handprint and orchestration of His flawless plan. Thank you for a life well lived that ignited a passion and hunger to know—really know—the Jesus you championed with your entire lives. In memory you are with me always. In essence, you have never gone away.

CONTENTS

FOREWORD

I'LL NEVER FORGET THE God-orchestrated way I met Lionel Mayell. The story begins when I was just eight years old. My parents and I were headed from Canada to Florida for a family vacation at Easter in 1966. Somehow our plane got re-routed and we ended up in St. Petersburg instead of Miami, with no hotel reservations at a peak vacation time. My mom decided we should take advantage of our warm, snow-less locale and go look at what a typical Florida home was like. I didn't know it then, but the trajectory of my entire life was about to change.

We drove around neighborhoods looking for houses for sale, and finally we came upon an open house that stood out like a used car lot, with flags flying all over the front lawn. Clearly someone knew how to market a home! Out from the house bounded a short, stout man with a great big smile and a pencil-thin moustache. His hand thrust out to shake ours. "Hi, I'm Lionel Mayell!" he said.

My mom found out that Lionel's wife and kids had already moved to California to begin working as missionaries with Campus Crusade for Christ. Since Lionel was by himself, my mom felt we should bring him a Kentucky Fried Chicken dinner that night. The first night turned into us bringing him dinner the next night and the next, thus creating chapter one in a story of our families lives intersecting on a pathway that has lasted to this very day.

At the end of the few days of dinners, Lionel wanted to return the favor, so he invited me to come meet his children in California. Upon visiting, it became quickly apparent that the contrast between our two homes was more than geographic. My home was one where religion was a battleground, with me as a young boy in the middle of a theological argument between my parents. Lionel's home, by contrast, was one where God was clearly at the center. Everyone agreed that was how it should be, and they built their lives around faith in God. I had no idea how to do that, but Lionel and his family did and they began to show me their ways.

As I got to know Lionel's family—his wife Dorothy, daughters Dottie and Rita, and son Carmen—I somehow became permanently embedded as the fourth child in the family. Over the years, I was taught how God mattered to everyday life. I was shown how the Bible was for daily life, not just a book to hear readings from in church once a week. I learned to love God deeply and practically, to love others sincerely, and I began sharing my newfound faith with others. Thanks to Lionel Mayell, I went from being a clueless church attender to a sold-out follower of Jesus Christ on a rock-solid foundation of truth I would never doubt. All because of one man named Lionel and the God he listened to, served, and modeled.

Some of my most thrilling yet terrifying memories involve Lionel's driving. Lionel was so short he could barely see over the steering wheel of his big Oldsmobile 98 sedan. On many days, he would be driving me up the curvy mountain roads to Campus Crusade, careening around the corners and straining to see, while telling me about yet another person he had introduced to Jesus. Whenever he told the story of a changed life, tears of joy would stream down his face, and he would look over at me for a bit too long and exclaim, "Isn't that wonderful, Greg? Rick found faith in Christ!" I remember feeling elated, yes, but equally nervous that Lionel would miss the next hairpin turn and we would all tumble down the hill.

It was on those winding roads I learned from Lionel to rejoice at the entrance of one life into the kingdom of God. To this day, I often cry at the news of someone finding faith in Jesus—I guess you could call them "Lionel Mayell tears." He taught me what really matters in life: it's who you bring with you to heaven to save them from missing out on a forever future with God.

In later years, my mom became ill with cancer, and it was Lionel and his family who helped her see God clearly and develop a relationship with Jesus. I'm grateful that because of Lionel and Dorothy, I'll see my mom again in heaven.

Like many business leaders before him, Lionel Mayell was a significant force in supporting church and nonprofit ministry causes. If it wasn't for Lionel, a young unknown preacher named Billy Graham would not have gotten his start in 1949; it was Lionel who stood up and championed Dr. Graham to preach at an evangelistic rally in Los Angeles in what was bitter-cold weather.

Today, I get to lead hundreds of Christian CEOs who work on their lives and businesses. Truth be told, I want them all to live like Lionel Mayell. He saw God clearly, saw himself accurately, and saw others in light of God's truth and lived to love them. I was fortunate enough to be one he loved for a long time.

You are going to enjoy learning about the life of Lionel Mayell. And maybe, just maybe, if you listen closely and let God orchestrate your life on His timetable, you too could be a Lionel Mayell for someone just like me—a lonely, motherless teenager who thought God was just a nice tack-on to the life he wanted for himself.

Has God brought a purposeless kid, a lonely neighbor, a hurting marriage, or a chance encounter across your path? By reaching into their life and practically caring about them, you just might change the trajectory of their lives. I'm praying that's what this book does as it fans out across the globe.

Greg Leith

CEO, Convene

www.convenenow.com

INTRODUCTION

I T HAD BEEN RAINING buckets since early morning, making roads treacherous and the climb up the winding mountain road to Arrowhead Springs Hotel almost impossible. Roads were flooded throughout Southern California, and the low cloud cover reduced visibility to near zero. Despite the pouring rain, cars lined up for miles on the roads leading to the Village Auditorium at the headquarters of Campus Crusade for Christ International. The Los Angeles City Council had even adjourned its session early in memory of one of the city's greatest citizens, Lionel Mayell.

The adrenaline rush that had revved me up for the last few days suddenly drained from my body as I was escorted to a seat in the front row. I was twenty, in my third year of college at Bible Institute of Los Angeles (now Biola University). My pulse quickened and my eyes filled with tears as I fixed my gaze on the picture on the easel, surrounded by three large white carnation crosses intertwined with red and white rosebuds. The man was my daddy. My hero. My giant.

Speaker after speaker took the podium to pay tribute to Dad. Some were household names in Christian circles, while others, like the former Hells Angel with tattoos covering all visible skin, probably made a few people uneasy. Each person talked about their personal experience with Dad and how he'd impacted their life. Dozens of personal messages were read aloud, including one from Billy Graham and one from Bob Pierce. But the message that spoke most to my heart that day, and the one that best captured the impact of Dad's life, was given by Dad's closest friend, Bill Bright, founder of Campus Crusade for Christ. He said:

> As I was thinking about this man, something came to my mind, and it kept coming back to me like a refrain: "There was a giant in the land and his name was Lionel Mayell. There was a giant in the land and his name was Lionel Mayell." I thought of several things that made this great man unique.
>
> He was a giant in his devotion to Christ. He loved the Lord Jesus supremely. We could not be together for more than a few minutes without having our conversation turn to the Lord Jesus Christ. Moments of praise, moments of prayer, moments of acknowledging His greatness.
>
> He was a giant in his devotion to his family. As we have heard from each of the children, he always put them first. He was a devoted father and husband. Wherever Lionel and Dorothy went, they exuded the supernatural love of the Lord Jesus.
>
> He was a giant in his witness to Christ. Because, as the apostle Paul said, "Wherever we go, we will tell everyone who will listen about Christ." And that was

Lionel Mayell. Wherever he went, there was someone in need of the Savior, and he was quick to tell them.

He was a giant in his desire to follow up and nurture new believers, as we heard today. Lionel took me under his wing and helped, encouraged, inspired, and instructed me.

He was a giant in his generosity, always giving, giving even when it meant doing without personally. Giving and encouraging others.

He was a giant in his vision and creativity. As some of you know, he was the father of the modern-day condominium. He pioneered this new concept many years ago, and it is still popular today.

Lionel Mayell was a giant, and there aren't a lot of giants in the land. Somehow, our modern society has a way of causing the masses to be satisfied with mediocrity, and Lionel was not satisfied to be an ordinary person. He was a giant.

Yes, there was a giant in the land, and his name was Lionel Mayell, and in the impression of his tracks will be observed his influence, which will be felt for many generations because he invented and used his money, his time, his influence, and his life where it resulted in multiplication hundreds of times over. I can almost feel his gentle hand on my shoulder as I speak. I can hear Lionel saying, "Enough. Don't talk about me. Talk about Jesus. Tell them about Jesus."

And if Dad were here today, that is what he would want me to tell you. He would want me to tell you about the Jesus he knew—the One who took up residence in Dad's heart when he was in his mid-forties; the One who erased every failure Dad had as a father and a husband; the One who, unbeknownst, wiped every tear from a scared little boy's eyes as he grieved his twelve-year-old brother; the One who replaced rejection with the unconditional acceptance and love that he had been seeking his entire life. That Jesus.

Dad's journey is a fascinating one. At only 5'2" in a world that equates appearance with success, he was often ridiculed and mocked. His mother told him that he was a mistake and would fail in life, and even rejected him in her death. He was given every reason to fail.

Dad set out to prove everyone wrong, and to gain the approval he so desperately needed. From a young age, he had one dream: to become wealthy. And that he did. He pioneered the first "own-your-own-apartment" homes on the West Coast and became known as the "Father of the Condominium" and the "Builder of Dreams." His ideas were so innovative that many of his projects are listed in the National Register of Historic Places.

His life was not without failures and mistakes, both personal and business. He was married and divorced twice. He squandered his millions in relentless pursuit of his own dream. But when he had an encounter with the person of Jesus Christ, it stopped him in his tracks and transformed how he thought, how he believed, how he approached every decision and obstacle he would face.

At a Youth for Christ meeting for teenagers, my forty-seven-year-old dad encountered the Savior who had loved him his entire life, the One who washed away all his mistakes and failures, the One who said, "I have a plan for your life. I'm for you. We'll do it together." It wasn't church. It wasn't religion. It was a *relationship*.

From that moment, Dad's passion focused not on making money, but on every person coming to know Jesus. He became convinced that God had the answer to every question he had, that He could solve every dilemma and wipe every tear. Dad's success in business skyrocketed, and his personal impact exploded as he caught God's dreams for the kingdom. He turned a $1,000 loan into a business empire worth $100 million and spanning four states, and he networked with some of the most significant waves of evangelism in the twentieth century.

This is the story of a little giant who God used to help change the world. Throughout Dad's failures and successes, and even before he was a Christian, the hand of a forgiving and loving God patiently wove the tapestry of his life to accomplish His overarching purpose. My hope is that you will find yourself in his story, be encouraged in your own journey, and realize that God wants to write your story to help change the world as well.

CHAPTER ONE

DIVINE ENCOUNTERS

IN THE SUMMER OF 1968, Daddy and I were dressed and in the car, waiting for Mom as we always did. The San Bernardino heat made the vinyl seats of our 1966 Oldsmobile sticky with our perspiration. I was ten years old.

Mom had made sure my hair was perfectly curled and that I was outfitted in a beautiful dress—as always. I made quite an appearance for her, but honestly, I felt more like a Raggedy Ann doll being dragged from place to place. Dressing-up to be on display for others was a new way of life for us, and I didn't like it.

After another ten minutes passed, Daddy said, "Ritalynn, run into the house and see if your mother needs help."

I jumped out of the car, ran up the concrete steps to the porch, and flung open the front door. Inside, Mom was counseling and encouraging whoever was on the other end of the phone. I waved my arms and flapped my hands, motioning that we had to go. She quickly ended her call with a prayer. That call had delayed us forty-five minutes.

Dad was scheduled to emcee at an important World Opportunities banquet in downtown Los Angeles, over an hour away. Now behind schedule, Mom made up the time by driving the sixty-plus miles between San Bernardino and LA in and out of traffic like a race-car driver while Dad prepared notes.

"Dorothy, darling, can you stop swerving?" he said. "I can't read my notes, and I'm getting dizzy looking down."

She exited the freeway and took a shortcut down a transitional street that had not been revitalized. From my spot in the backseat, I heard the door locks snap into place and saw her glance around to ensure the windows were rolled up.

"Look, Mother!" Daddy yelled. "Did you see that man on the side of the road?"

I groaned.

Mom said nothing.

"Darling, did you see that man on the side of the road?" he repeated.

"Yes, Lionel, but we're running late and need to get you to the banquet," she replied.

"Mother, don't you trust the Lord? It will only take a minute."

"Oh, Lionel, why do you always have to *see*?" She sighed and slowed down, then circled back and pulled up to the curb near where the ragged-looking homeless man sat. "Please hurry."

Dad barreled out of the car toward him. The man was either tanned or dirty, dressed in layers of grimy, old clothing. He appeared to have lived on the streets his whole life. A shopping cart full of his rag-tag possessions sat close beside him.

Mom and I watched Dad struggle with his old knees to stoop and sit with him on the curb. There was Dad in his expensive tailored suit and tie next to a man unshaven and dressed in tattered clothes. I wondered why he wore so many layers in the summer heat.

Daddy did not care about the man's appearance or odor, or who he was or even what he'd done to get in such dire straits. He saw people differently from the rest of us. We sat there with the car running for at least fifteen minutes while they engaged in what seemed to be a riveting personal conversation.

Dad leaned forward to make eye contact. Passersby paused to stare, and many took a second look. Dad didn't notice; his gaze was fixed on the man's wizened face. Slowly, the homeless man stood and helped Daddy to his feet. They locked arms around each other in a fierce hug. Daddy pointed to the car.

Mom groaned. "I knew this was going to happen."

Daddy tapped on the rolled-up window, brandishing a big grin. "Dorothy, meet Stephen, your new brother in the Lord! He needs shelter. Do you remember where the mission is?"

Mom gave Dad one of those looks as if to say, "Lionel, what are you thinking?" But instead, she smiled and nodded. "Stephen, so nice to meet you."

I laughed inside at my mother's predicament—until Stephen slid into the backseat next to me.

The odor of alcohol, smoke, and days' or weeks' worth of body odor filled the car. Mom rolled down the windows.

As it was, she didn't know how to get to the mission from where we were. After asking several people for directions, we finally arrived at the LA Union Mission. Dad took Stephen inside, paid for a week's stay, and made sure he had what he needed.

By the time we got to the banquet, the guests had already started the dessert course. Dad walked briskly to the platform and apologized for being late. He paused, laid aside his prepared notes, and then, instead of his planned speech, shared his burden for the homeless man whom he met on the way to the banquet.

Several weeks later, I learned that a connection Dad knew from that banquet had heard the story and went to the mission afterward and hired Stephen. He let him live in their guest house while doing landscaping work. It turned out that Stephen was a skilled landscaper who had lost his family and turned to alcohol. As was typical with Daddy, he always saw the potential in a person—not their current situation or condition.

Growing up in the 1960s, what Dad did that day stood out to me. That was the way he lived his life. It was just like him to hold up a banquet for the rich and famous to stop for one man who'd lost his dream.

In his heart of hearts, Dad was a dream-builder. Newspapers in the 1950s called him the "Father of the Condominium" and the "Builder of Dreams" because he pioneered the 1920s-era Long Beach projects, including the still-famous Villa Riviera, Cooper Arms, and Artaban. He designed and built the Whispering Waters condominiums in Texas, Florida, and California, the Villa San Pasqual in Pasadena, Villa del Coronado in Phoenix, and Villa Catalina in Tucson, Arizona.

Dad was known for the way he landscaped too. He brought the outside in with lush, beautiful gardens and water features that served a dual purpose; in addition to the aesthetics, they also cooled the building's air conditioning system by recirculation through specialized equipment. Dad designed the first glass elevator and used marble countertops in the 1940s and 1950s, before anyone else had thought of either.

Born in 1897, by the time he was twenty-four, Dad had made his first million—all before the Great Depression. He understood the thrill of living his dream, but he also poured into the dreams of others and, more importantly, tapped into the dream of God.

Years into his career, he had an encounter with God in the person of Jesus Christ at a Youth for Christ event where he'd taken his teenage children. He heard for the first time the message that transformed his heart. What had once been a religious belief that God *could* became an inward conviction that God *would*.

From that day forward, God worked in and through Dad to powerfully network some of the most significant waves of evangelism in the twentieth century, including Billy Graham's first-ever Los Angeles crusade.

Dad liked to tell a little-known story. His blue eyes sparkled with joy as he recalled the remarkable answer to prayer that took place to make the crusade happen, and how powerfully it demonstrated God's goodness and greatness.

In 1946, most people had never heard of Billy Graham. Torrey Johnson, a well-known Chicago-based evangelist and the first president of Youth for Christ International, had just returned from England where Billy, Youth for Christ's (YFC) first full-time evangelist, was drawing extraordinary crowds at rallies across Europe. Torrey was staying in our home in Los Angeles, and shared something important with Dad: "Lionel, I've never seen such altar calls in my life. I believe this young Billy Graham will become the greatest living evangelist in America."

At the time, Dad was on the board of directors of Christ for Greater Los Angeles, a diverse group of Christian businessmen who desired revival for their city, and was responsible for selecting speakers who could attract thousands of people to hear the gospel during annual revival meetings. Being such a large city,

Los Angeles routinely drew crowds of around eighteen thousand people and attracted the most famous evangelists of the times.

After listening to Torrey, Dad presented the name of Billy Graham to the board at a meeting to determine who would be the speaker for the 1947 annual revival meeting.

Opposition was outspoken.

"Why, he's not even known!" one director exclaimed.

"We can't use a young man like this man Billy Graham, who is inexperienced and unknown around the world," another chimed in. "We can't use him in a sophisticated city like Los Angeles. He couldn't draw anybody to a great crusade. We need to have a well-known evangelist who can draw crowds."

Another board member said, "If the board of directors should undertake to accept this proposal, the danger of financial involvement would be so great that they would have to resign."

Dad wasn't about to give up. "Gentlemen," he said, drawing his spare frame up to full stature, "the precious Holy Spirit can bring the crowds. With the right kind of publicity by us, with each one of us inspired by the Holy Spirit, we can have capacity attendance and see Christ uplifted."

The vote was cast. The directors voted to wait until Billy Graham became better known.

Deep inside, though, Dad had caught the dream of God. He knew that God wanted Billy Graham to preach in Los Angeles. Undaunted, he went before the board of directors of Youth for Christ of Los Angeles, where he was also a board member. Every year, they had a big rally in the great Shrine Auditorium, but that year they had been discussing switching to the Hollywood Bowl, which would hold double the capacity.

"Again I presented the name of Billy Graham to the board," Dad recalled when repeating his story, "and the Holy Spirit took my words. The board approved and invited young Billy Graham to be the speaker at a one-night rally in the Hollywood Bowl."

The night for this great meeting arrived in the summer of 1947. Even before opening, the Hollywood Bowl was packed to the perimeter.

"There must have been seventeen thousand people there!" Dad recounted. And at the close of Billy Graham's great message, hundreds poured down the aisles and climbed over seats to reach the altar. Over one thousand people received Jesus Christ as Savior that night. The city of Los Angeles had never seen anything like it.

Immediately following this great Youth for Christ gathering, the Christ for Greater Los Angeles board called a special meeting. This time the decision was unanimous to invite Billy Graham to return in the fall of 1949 for the great citywide revival. That revival would end up being the greatest evangelistic crusade in the history of the United States. It launched Billy Graham into national prominence.

In September of 1949, the historic meeting opened. It was held under a large Ringling Brothers circus tent, often referred to as the Canvas Cathedral with the Steeple of Light. Erected on the corner of Washington and Hill Streets, the mammoth tent held 6,600 seats. Billy Graham's team included George Beverly Shea as soloist, Cliff Barrows as music director, and evangelist brothers T. W. and Grady Wilson.

God's dream was realized. Dad was thrilled. But his faith was about to be tested like never before.

That September, the Los Angeles area experienced the coldest weather ever recorded. Winds were penetrating. The flaps of the huge tent had to be spiked to the ground to anchor the tent's rafters, and several large gas heaters were installed. Although advertised extensively, the meetings seldom drew more than 2,500 people because of the severe cold. Yet the altar calls were like nothing that had ever been seen.

Finally, the last day of the revival arrived. The preceding three weeks had completed the original contracted time frame for the campaign. Although attendance was spotty due to the weather, the Lord had met all expenses. Many were on the verge of inviting Christ into their hearts.

The board of directors met to discuss whether the revival would continue. No one wanted to be responsible for closing the meetings, although some did fear bankruptcy if they continued. Billy Graham had never held a campaign longer than three weeks and he had few sermons left, but he was willing to stay from week to week if the board so desired.

At 7:20 p.m., hundreds of people rushed into the tent for what was supposed to be the final service. The air was tense. At only 5'2", Dad had to stand during the board meeting so he could be seen. He made a motion that was immediately seconded and passed unanimously.

He told them, "Gentlemen, seemingly the bad weather has destroyed our faith. We know that Satan does not want these great meetings to continue. God has given us great preaching through Billy Graham. The Lord has proven to us His great pleasure with the fruit of Billy's ministry, for even with the small crowds we've had, the greatest altar calls have been made, and we've never seen such response. The Lord controls all things."

He continued, "Well, do we remember that Christ broke up the storm on the lake when the boat began to sink? He is our great Lord and Savior and does not wish that any should perish, but that all should be brought to salvation. Therefore, I move that if our great and mighty Lord should see fit to change the weather this night within one hour from now, when Billy will just about be closing his sermon, if there is a noticeable change in the weather, Billy will be authorized to announce that the meetings will continue week to week, as the Lord leads."

Before 8:20 on that Sunday evening, as Billy closed his sermon, people all over the tent began to fan themselves with anything that was handy. Billy paused in his sermon to ask the engineers to turn off the heaters and have the ushers put up the tent flaps to allow the ocean breeze in. Someone struck up the song "Praise God from Whom All Blessings Flow." The whole tent was electrified.

"A miracle has taken place before our very eyes," Billy Graham announced. "This great crusade will continue for at least another week, and for as long as the Holy Spirit continues to look on these meetings with favor."

A collective cheer erupted from the crowd, but no one cheered louder than Lionel Mayell. From that night on, the weather was favorable, and the crusade was extended for a total of eight weeks. Thousands more decisions for Christ were recorded from that night forward.

Among the new converts was California's most popular radio personality, Stuart Hamblen; former mafia wire-tapper Jim Vaus;

infamous gangster and racketeer Mickey Cohen; and Olympic distance runner and war hero Louis Zamperini.

Hamblen was America's first singing cowboy, and after his conversion, he became well known for enduring classics such as "It Is No Secret (What God Can Do)" and "This Ole House," which was popularized by Rosemary Clooney and later sung by both Elvis and Willie Nelson. Zamperini was one of the most celebrated American servicemen of World War II. His amazing story of survival and enduring torture in Japanese POW camps became the subject of the best-selling book by Laura Hillenbrand and recent motion picture, *Unbroken*, directed and produced by Angelina Jolie.

The crusade was a flurry of activity. Reporters were on hand to cover every meeting. Billy Graham made three to four speaking appearances per day and gave dozens of interviews.

After a while, he needed a place to get away from the crowds. Mom and Dad opened their home to him and his team during the first few weeks. Theirs was a stately home at the intersection of June Street and Wilshire Boulevard, in the exclusive Hancock Park section of Los Angeles.

Nestled on a shy one acre and set far back from the street, my parents' 1926 Spanish Mediterranean estate had lush, exquisitely landscaped grounds and a separate guest quarters, ample room to provide a comfortable homey retreat from the busy crusade for Billy Graham and his team.

Dad was sensitive to Billy's need for down time and reflection so he could study for his sermons, pray, and recharge. He arranged for all communication and phone calls to be routed through him in the main house to protect Billy and the team from the onslaught of attention. Every hospitality was extended to make them feel welcome. Eventually, however, people discovered where they were staying, and Billy and his team were forced to move to a hotel for the last six weeks of the crusade.

Almost every night during those last weeks, Mom and Dad hosted parties in their home to encourage new Christians. Many Christian Hollywood celebrities attended to share their testimonies, such as Roy Rogers and Dale Evans, singer/actor Redd Harper, youth evangelist Jack Wyrtzen of Word of Life Camp, and Stuart Hamblen and Louis Zamperini. Even Roy Rogers' horse, Trigger, came to their home for a visit.

My parents focused on how to encourage and build up new believers. Little did they know that those parties were all a part of God's overarching plan of preparing and cultivating His dreams and purposes for them.

————

God used Dad in the 1949 Billy Graham meetings, and as a mighty influence in the callings of others. When Dad acted upon his intense desire for the people of Los Angeles to know Jesus, God was already orchestrating each encounter, connection, and relationship as part of His plan for Dad's future. Much later, Dad told me, "Ritalynn, God has never forgotten your daddy."

While riding in the car to the banquet that day, as a ten-year-old girl, I did not understand why he would take time to stop for a homeless man. Yet those acts of grace became a familiar pattern that I witnessed throughout my life. Dad counted it as much of a privilege to sit with a homeless man as he did to speak on a platform in a banquet hall or an auditorium full of ministry celebrities and major donors. He had a different way of seeing people. As he took every opportunity to outwardly demonstrate God's love, he modeled God's heart to me. For Dad, the object of ministry was in every "chance" encounter with every person along the way. He didn't have to run "to" ministry; he was living it.

Dad trusted his heavenly Father with every detail of his life. It took me many years to learn to do this for myself. But in the same way that God orchestrated every encounter to fashion and shape Dad's future, He was also using every life experience I had to shape and prepare me—even on that day when Dad stopped for one man who'd lost his dream.

"Am I the Mother of This Thing?"

U NA MAYELL ASKED TO see her newborn son. It was
February 4, 1897, in the early hours of a snowy morning
in London, Ontario, Canada. Leon (later changed to Lionel)
Vincent Mayell was born before the use of incubators for babies,
and at four pounds, he was pale, blue, and pathetically skinny.
The nurse tenderly wrapped the baby boy in a hospital blanket
and placed him in his mother's arms.

Una lifted the edge of the blanket, squinted, and looked up
at the nurse. "Am I the mother of this thing? It's more monkey
than man!" Her disappointment gave way to tears, and she cried
inconsolably.

"Oh, Mrs. Mayell, please don't cry," the nurse said as she
patted her arm. "We've had even uglier babies than yours come
out of this hospital and live a normal life. You'll learn to love him
just as though he was very beautiful."

What the nurse didn't know was that Una had lost her infant daughter, Margaret, seven years earlier and her grief for her firstborn only compounded her disappointment in giving birth to an unsightly premature baby. Later that day, the baby's father, Arthur Wellesley Mayell, went to the viewing window, where he was more chagrined than proud. Distressed by their son's size and appearance, he and Una took him home and wrapped him in rolls of cotton batting, then laid him in one of their dresser drawers.

Little Lionel was a colicky baby, crying so much that his parents were asked to move from boarding house after boarding house because he was disturbing the other boarders. For the first two years of his life, they were asked to pack up and move about every two weeks. The doctor told them, "You'll just have to endure it and let him cry himself out."

It wasn't until Lionel was almost three years old that he was big enough to be weighed on a regular scale and to sleep in a regular bed instead of a dresser drawer. Greatly concerned about appearances, Una told her small son on several occasions, "You were a mistake." Her words struck the core of his heart.

When Lionel was five, the Mayell family welcomed a new baby boy into the family—Carman Wellesley Mayell, who quickly became the object of his parents' attention and affection. They beamed with pride when young Carman announced that he wanted to be a missionary when he grew up.

Although Lionel was the older brother, he soon found himself falling behind Carman in more ways than one. Carman was "all boy," a sharp, athletic kid who beat his older brother in all the races. The boys loved each other, but as boys often do, they liked to challenge one another's strength.

"Come on, Lionel, take me on! Come on, let me have it. Give me your best shot!" Carman would persist until Lionel agreed and came at him full force. Carman was stronger, and he proved several times that he could throw Lionel down and sit on him in three minutes flat.

One day, Lionel met his father at the door when he got home from work. "Dad," he said, "Carman constantly buffets me about. He knocks me over, wrestles with me, sits on me, and won't let me breathe."

"Why don't you do some exercise?" his father answered gruffly. "You're ten years old and he's five. He ought not to be able to throw you around and beat you in all the races and everything else."

Lionel tried, but his brother was already taller than he was. Only weeks before, Lionel had walked under the dining room table without hitting his head on the underside of the table.

Lionel was twelve when his father decided to sell his lucrative wholesale grocery business in Ontario, Canada, and move to Southern California. California was the land of opportunity in 1909, but it was the several-thousand-mile journey by rail on the old Santa Fe that forever changed the lives of the Mayell family.

The desert heat scorched as they reached California, with temperatures often soaring over one hundred degrees. With no air conditioning and only open windows for ventilation, the boys made frequent trips to the tanks that carried drinking water and ice for the passengers. Using tin cups as containers, Lionel and Carman drank cup after cup of the ice-filled water to get relief from the heat.

Several days later, they arrived at the home of Una's parents, a wealthy couple living in the fashionable West Adams district of Los Angeles, under the eaves of the University of Southern California. South Flower Street was a neighborhood of large, ornate two- and three-story houses, and home to Los Angeles's most successful entrepreneurs. Three doors to the north were the Robinsons, of the Robinson's Department Store empire. Next to them were George Ralphs, founder of the Ralphs Grocery Company, and John Haggerty, founder of Haggerty's Department Stores.

After their arrival in Los Angeles, Carman became seriously ill. His wealthy grandfather retained the finest physicians possible, and the doctors told Una that her son's intestines were "paralyzed." He had apparently contracted dysentery from drinking the ice water on their long trip to California. The prognosis was grim.

For eleven months, Carman was unable to eat; all his nutrition was provided intravenously. He became emaciated, like a starving child with a distended stomach, prominent cheek bones, and tight yellow skin. He was a living skeleton. Lionel's heart was broken. After eleven months of suffering, their parents were frantic. They sought every way possible to restore their son's health, even turning to faith healing.

Pentecostal evangelist Finis Yoakum had gained widespread fame as the leading apostle of the faith-healing movement in Los Angeles. Desperate for answers, Una transported Carman to Yoakum's Pisgah Faith Home in the Highland Park section, a sanatarium-type establishment where "inmates" were prayed over and instructed in the Bible.

After Dr. Yoakum prayed over Carman, he proclaimed the boy healed and ordered that he be fed steak, potatoes, salad, and lemon pie (Carman's favorite meal). He ate solid food for the first time in months, but during the night he began having convulsions. Just before dawn the next morning, Carman passed away.

That night, Lionel felt torn spiritually and emotionally. He heard his mother sobbing a few rooms away and his father gruffly trying to calm her. The conversation got loud.

"I wish it could have been Leon!" she wailed. "Why couldn't it have been Leon that died?" In her bitterness over losing her favorite son, Una pierced the heart of her only living child. Her words stung deeply.

Lionel loved his brother, and watching him slowly die had been difficult to bear. He was utterly alone now. But nothing could be done. Carman was gone. And Lionel couldn't help wondering where his brother was now.

Lionel drifted off to sleep, his pillow wet with tears. During the night, he had a vivid dream of a field of daisies and a young boy running toward him with his arms outstretched. As he ran, the boy called, "Leon! Leon!"

Carman!

Carman's body was perfect and whole, with a radiant glow coming from his face. Lionel woke up, his heart comforted, and he felt a supernatural peace. He knew that Carman was with God, and that God had granted him this vision.

Lionel's parents were inconsolable. Just two days after Carman died, the faith healer who had prayed over him came to visit Una. "Mrs. Mayell," he proclaimed, "God took your son home because of your lack of faith."

Una cried inconsolably for hours, repeating, "It was my lack of faith that crucified my son!" The whole family seemed to be falling apart. But in his heart, Lionel clung to the dream that God had given him the night after Carman died.

The following years were tough for Lionel. Arthur was a strict disciplinarian of English background, good-looking, brilliant in his business, and driven. At only 5'6", he wasn't a tall man, but he would become very angry if Lionel didn't do something he wanted. He would yell and sometimes punish Lionel severely. On one occasion, Arthur beat his legs with a big stick almost to the point of breaking them. When Una intervened, he grabbed her with both hands and so strained her muscles that she ended up swollen and bruised.

Arthur and Una Mayell moved with Lionel from her parents' home to a beautiful house in Long Beach, California. One day a friend called on Una and invited her to attend a Bible study in a lovely home on the main boulevard. That night she found the inner peace she so desperately sought, and accepted Jesus as her personal Savior. In that moment, she came to understand that Carman's death was *not* due to her lack of faith.

Una was a striking woman from a very wealthy family, highly educated and intelligent, with an impressive vocabulary and a captivating personality. She became enthralled with the Word of God and immersed herself in the study of Greek and Hebrew, becoming one of the first students to enroll in the Bible Institute of Los Angeles (now Biola University). After her conversion, she was one of the most highly sought-after Christian speakers in Southern California, an accomplished debater, and a writer for Christian magazines all over the country.

Upon the invitation of W. E. Biederwolf, a fiery but scholarly evangelist during the same era as Billy Sunday, she joined his evangelistic team. Separate meetings were held for women, and Una would teach and organize the follow-up work across the country. Often, after she spoke to women at his Sunday-afternoon services, phenomenal altar calls brought scores of people to the front to receive Jesus as Savior.

Una's fine biblical expositions and writings won her wide acclaim, and she enjoyed entertaining their many friends and colleagues. Evangelist R. A. Torrey lived just one block away in Long Beach and was a close friend and regular visitor in the Mayell home. He had moved to Los Angeles to start the Bible Institute of Los Angeles in the tradition of Moody Bible Institute in Chicago, and served as the school's first dean and the pastor of its Church of the Open Door. Other frequent guests included such Christian leaders of the day as Edwin Orr, Gipsy Smith, Louis Talbot of Talbot Seminary, Cortland Myers, Henrietta Mears, Arthur Pink, Charles Fuller of Fuller Seminary, and Charles Woodbridge.

Una was a mesmerizing figure for her time, and she used her considerable persuasiveness to ensure that Lionel got saved. She made sure he was sharply dressed and highly educated, and that he impressed the Christian leaders she entertained in her home. She had him baptized using three different methods—once by dipping his head forward three times, another by immersion, and a third by sprinkling. When that didn't encourage him to accept Christ, she devised another plan—to make him learn Greek and translate the New Testament. She hired a well-known Greek scholar and supervised Lionel in the study of Greek for five years.

Nothing worked, and although he retained and even practiced many of the principles he learned, it was not until later that he came to have a personal relationship with Jesus Christ.

Not much is known about Arthur Mayell's conversion experience. He was a dynamic businessman who professed to be a

Christian and served on the board of every church his family attended. In 1912, he became Public Relations Officer for Foreign Affairs in California. Anytime royalty from Canada or England visited the state, Arthur and Una would entertain them. His fortune skyrocketed in the early 1920s when he quite literally struck it rich by drilling oil wells in the famous Signal Hill area of Long Beach, but he subsequently lost a fortune when he moved drilling to Texas just before his death, in 1925, at age sixty.

Both Arthur and Una were high-achievers and they traveled extensively, Arthur throwing himself into his business and Una "serving the Lord." As a teenager, Lionel raised himself. He didn't have parents who told him that he mattered and cheered him on. He was like a little David in a Goliath world, facing every giant alone.

But Lionel treasured in his heart that God had reached out to him in a dream the night after his brother died, and deep down he knew there was a God who cared about him. The many Christian leaders who came to his home became friends and powerful spiritual influences in his life, stimulating his desire and motivating him to dream God's dreams for his own life.

————

All I ever heard growing up was that Dad had been raised in a home where they entertained the who's-whos of the Christian world. Because I had never heard Dad say one unkind thing about his parents, I assumed all was happy in his boyhood home. Dad's parents didn't know the Lord during his early years, and the Enemy used all the hurtful things his parents spoke to try to discourage him.

But Dad's vision of his brother was a supernatural seed planted in his heart by a loving God. He knew Dad needed encouragement, and what Satan meant for evil, God turned around for good. Perhaps it was the intense rejection he faced as a child that gave Dad a unique sensitivity, as an adult, to be able to understand and read others' hearts. He came to know that people look "on the outward appearance, but the LORD looks on the heart" (1 Samuel 16:7 ESV).

THE FATHER OF THE CONDOMINIUM

FIFTEEN-YEAR-OLD LIONEL MAYELL STRIPPED down to his skivvies and crawled under the big two-story house in Long Beach with a hoe in his hand. He had begged and pleaded with his parents to let him get a summer job. While he didn't need to work, he was bored and eager to do something. Anything. This was the perfect job—a house-moving company needed someone just his size to crawl under the house and dig out a trench so the large timbers could be inserted under the house's framing to lift it.

"Dig a trench the entire width of the house," the foreman shouted, "at least a foot deep and just as wide." Oil-well timbers would be used to lift the house off its framing, and then big floating timbers would be used to move it off the site and down the street.

Lionel did his best, crawling on all fours and carving as deep into the sandy silt as he could. Progress was slow, hot, difficult, and boring. He didn't get many breaks, but talked to the other workers around him to pass the time.

At the end of his first day, the foreman wasn't happy. "Mayell, you talk too much. You talk more than you work. We're going to pay you for the first day's work, but don't come back." Just like that, his first job was over.

Thinking that maybe digging trenches wasn't his forte, the next summer Lionel sought a job at a large olive- and tuna-packing plant in Long Beach, the Curtis Corporation. Making 25 cents an hour, his job was to carry the large tuna from the furnaces to the tables where women sat cutting the fish into pieces and packing it into small cans.

It was a smelly, dirty job, and offered little experience for learning to run a business. Still, the job worked out well and Lionel returned to work at the Curtis packing plant for the next two summers before he went off to college. (He was surprised when years later, during Prohibition in 1923, his former employer was arrested for bootlegging by stashing crates of liquor underneath the large cargoes of tuna brought into the harbor.)

As Lionel considered what to study in college, his mother had her own plans. Una believed he should become a minister, so she took him along when she taught Bible lessons at First Presbyterian Church of Hollywood and First Presbyterian Church of Long Beach, introducing him to all the important people. She made connections for him to work in the evangelical campaigns of Billy Sunday and Gipsy Smith, even entertaining Billy Sunday in their Long Beach home.

He gained a lot of head knowledge during those years, and even thought of himself as a "Christian," but he never truly opened his heart to Jesus Christ. He was stubborn. In her frustration, Una lashed out with an all-too-common reminder: "Lionel, you're nothing but a little runt, and without Christ in your life, you'll be a failure. You'll never be able to compete with real men. The best job you can ever expect to get will be a street-cleaning job." Although he admired his mother and knew she wanted the best for him, he couldn't help but feel the sting of rejection. Deep inside, he steeled his resolve to succeed.

Despite his mother's gloomy predictions, Lionel excelled academically and, in 1916, received a scholarship to Occidental College through the assistance of A. W. Buell, one of the college's trustees and a family friend. Occidental was a small liberal arts college in the Eagle Rock neighborhood of Los Angeles, and was often referred to as the "Princeton of the West." Lionel was excited to experience college life, be away from home, and meet his new classmates.

Founded by a group of Presbyterian clergy and laymen, Occidental was the college of choice for many Christian families. With an enrollment of only five hundred students, Lionel found it easy to make new friends, many of whom would remain friends for life. He enjoyed the long and intense discussions with his roommate, a quiet third-year student named Cameron Townsend, who would later become the founder of Wycliffe Bible Translators. Another roommate was all-American athlete Louis Evans Sr., who went on to be a senior pastor at First Presbyterian Church of Hollywood. Sam Sutherland was a long-time friend and classmate who would later become the fifth president of Biola University and president of the Lockman Foundation.

Although surrounded by strong Christian influences, Lionel still did not become a Christian. What he did become was a driven man, focused on high performance and determined to succeed in his own right.

Right after graduation, Lionel set his sights on becoming a lawyer, enrolling in the College of Law at the University of Southern California in downtown Los Angeles. He accelerated his studies by taking both day and night classes. For two years, he left his home in Long Beach at 7 a.m. every day, taking the Pacific Electric streetcar to the Tajo law building of the University of Southern California at 1st and Broadway, returned home in the afternoon to study for a few hours, and then rode back downtown for night classes until about 9:30. After that, he enrolled in Stanford Law School near Palo Alto, and it was here during his study of case law that he began to develop an innovative new concept in multi-family housing.

During his study of contract law, Lionel became enthralled with the great cooperative apartments being built in New York City and other large cities on the East Coast. In those days, apartment buildings were legally owned by a corporation. The interested buyer bought stock in the corporation, and the corporation then gave the buyer the rights to their apartment in the form of a lease issued for a term of ninety-nine years. It was called "ownership" but was not true ownership; it was merely a lease by the corporation.

About the same time, Lionel received a newsletter from the Long Beach Chamber of Commerce, reporting that thousands of winter tourists from back East were flocking to the booming

California seaside resort following the end of World War I. Before World War II, nearly all visitors to American resorts, including those staying for an entire season, lived either in hotels or furnished rental apartments.[1] With such an influx of tourists, there were not enough hotels or apartments to house them, and the city of Long Beach was actually promoting the building of cooperative apartments.

Lionel's interest piqued. But he knew that this style of stock cooperative would never succeed in California, not after what happened there during World War I. Several high-profile city-center projects had failed—either the developer disappeared with people's deposits or they couldn't generate enough interest.[2] Countless others had gone into bankruptcy because they couldn't get materials to build during the war. He knew that no one would buy apartments on a stock basis for fear that they would lose them, and was sure he had the solution to the problem. But it had never been done before.

In 1919, while on spring break from Stanford, Lionel, bursting with excitement over his newfound idea, went to visit an old friend of his father. State senator Newton Thompson was now the title officer and assistant manager of Title Insurance and Trust Company of Los Angeles, Southern California's oldest trust company.

"Senator, I'm Arthur Mayell's son, and I just left Stanford University," Lionel told him. "I want to build apartment buildings, but I don't want to build them on the cooperative plan because that's a lease plan and stock plan. People in California who have experienced defunct corporations during the war won't be interested in buying apartments on a stock basis. However, I believe I can sell apartments on a feasible-deed basis."

Senator Thompson leaned over his desk. "Mayell, I've never heard of anything like that before—selling apartments or owning apartments in which the title company will give a policy of insurance, guaranteed by the Title Insurance and Trust Company."

"Well, would you study the situation and then get back to me and advise me, please?"

"Fine, fine," he said. "I'd be glad to. Come back in a couple of weeks, and I'll let you know."

Lionel smiled and shook his hand. Two weeks later, he returned to Senator Thompson's office.

"Mayell, you really struck them on a good deal," the senator said. "I've never heard of it. But you certainly can sell apartments on a deed basis. Even more than that, I presented it to my board of directors, and they've prepared a contract to give to you. They will give a policy of title insurance on any apartment you sell in your buildings."

He continued, "Now here's the plan that you'd have to adopt. You buy the property that you want to build a building on. You'll deed the property in trust to the Title Insurance and Trust Company of Los Angeles. You'll have your attorneys draw up the declaration of trust, which we will sign and you will sign. And you'll deliver to us the deed to the property and to the building in which you are selling the apartments. When you sell an apartment, we will issue a policy of title insurance on that apartment, guaranteeing that the apartment is clear and free from every lien and encumbrance."

Lionel tried not to grin from ear to ear.

"Lionel, you're about to do something that has never been done, and you should make millions of dollars on that plan. Go do it!"

The ride home to Long Beach on the street car seemed to take only a few minutes. Over and over he rehearsed the words he would use to explain his idea to his parents, share the news from Senator Thompson, and ask to borrow enough money to get his idea off the ground.

Arthur and Una Mayell both had savvy business minds, and initially they tried to discourage him.

"It's a true 'own-your-own' apartment," Lionel explained. "The buyer gets a warranty deed to his home, a full and complete legal title just like he would if it were a single-family home. You don't rent it, you own it. And you're free to resell it if you want, remodel it the way you want, or leave it to your children, without any corporation telling you what you can do. I can make it work. I've already got the property picked out overlooking the ocean, and I've got the Title Insurance and Trust Company to back up my idea."

Even at the young age of twenty-two, he understood something about human nature better than others: people like to own their own space. Early on, he recognized the symbolic value of the deed in conveying a greater level of freedom and individuality than renting.[3] It had strong emotional appeal, elevating a buyer above a renter, and allowed comparison to owning a house.

Still skeptical but wanting to support their son, the Mayells agreed to take out a loan against the family home to help Lionel get his project off the ground. With the $500 he borrowed from his mother, he bought a ninety-day option on some land. He was so sure that his cooperative apartments would be successful, that he put all his effort and energy into the project, despite discouragement from his elders. Following up on prospects by bicycle, he became a familiar sight riding through the streets of Long Beach day and night.

By December 1, 1919, Lionel had sold a mere $15,000 in apartments, and the land owners notified him that he needed to double that amount in thirty days or he would lose the option on the property. Lionel called in a favor, contacting a banker whose lawn he had cut for no charge as a boy, and he asked him to give him a list of clients who had at least $5,000 on savings deposit. It was an unorthodox thing to do, but Lionel said nothing about the bank when he called upon the clients. Within thirty days, he had sold $750,000 worth of apartments to the bank's clients and saved the option. Having found his passion, he left Stanford Law School one month shy of graduation in 1920.

Lionel established the offices of Mayell Enterprises on Ocean Boulevard in Long Beach. The preliminary plans for his first proposed nine-story building were completed, and the architect's rendering of it sat in the center of his office display window. His advertising campaign was ready. He had gotten this far without having had any previous business or construction experience, any training in buying materials or planning buildings, or any sales experience. And although he wasn't yet a Christian, he found inspiration in the story of John Wanamaker, the nation's first postmaster general and the builder of one of the largest department store chains in the country.

John Wanamaker had started his career as a simple office boy, but he became a wealthy, successful businessman and a fine Christian. On his desk was a bronze plaque with the Bible verse he built his life around, Hebrews 11:6: "Without faith it is impossible to please him, but he that cometh unto God must believe that He is and that He is a rewarder of they that diligently seek him."

Lionel liked the reward part, and decided to claim that as his life verse. He fully believed that if he continually sought God's leading in his life and his business, God would reward him.

Whenever prospective purchasers came to meet with him in his office, he would go into a closet or some private room and thank the Lord for all past answers to his prayers and God's many ways of guiding his business. He would quote Hebrews 11:6, and pray, "Now, Lord, I'm calling on you to make me successful and to teach me in the way I should go, how I am to build buildings, how I am to sell apartments, how I am to advertise them. Dear Lord, I can do nothing without your help. You have promised to reward me."

In every respect, it seemed that God did indeed reward Mayell Enterprises. By 1922, Lionel had completed the first own-your-own apartment house on the West Coast on his deed plan. The Artaban, a nine-story luxury building in Long Beach with a $2 million value, which he both financed and built, was the first of many projects throughout the 1920s that earned him the reputation as the successful pioneer of the own-your-own-apartment concept and later, in the 1950s and 1960s, the "Father of the Condominium."

By 1929, Lionel had developed, financed, constructed, and sold cooperative apartments on the deed plan in Los Angeles and Long Beach, totaling $10 million. Newspaper articles and letters from business associates from that time describe him as a man of great energy, unusual executive ability, and integrity. He possessed an extraordinary talent for promoting his projects and a persuasiveness that ensured prospective buyers, investors, bankers, and underwriters of its certain success.

The own-your-own apartment quickly came into widespread regional use, and at least half of Southern California's cooperatively owned apartment houses before the Great Depression were own-your-owns rather than stock cooperatives.[4] Many of Lionel's buildings still stand today as monuments to his vision and skill, and have achieved landmark status and historic significance.

When construction began on the Cooper Arms in 1923, a *Los Angeles Times* article described it as "an apartment house which, when completed, will become one of the most imposing structures of its kind west of Chicago." At that time, the Long Beach skyline lacked other skyscrapers. The *Times* went on to predict that "this magnificent building will become a landmark that may be seen from ocean vessels miles away."[5]

When completed in 1924, Cooper Arms was the largest and most expensive cooperative to date, a luxury high-rise in the Period Revival style with Italian Renaissance and Classical Revival architectural features. In 1980, it was one of the first buildings to be designated a Long Beach Historical Landmark, and it achieved National Register Historic status in 2000.

Long Beach's preeminent landmark and "the building that helped define the city" is the majestic Villa Riviera, completed in 1929 at a cost of $2.75 million. Conceived and developed by Lionel Mayell and designed by a local architect, the sixteen-story Gothic Revival beachfront high-rise won grand prize in an international architectural competition and was the second-tallest building in Southern California.

A full-page spread of the Villa Riviera in the 1929 issue of *Architectural Digest* put Long Beach on the architectural map of the West Coast. Its apartments sold for between $12,000 and $50,000 in 1929, about $172,000 to $720,000 in today's dollars. Buyers were attracted to its architectural distinction, beachfront location, and luxurious amenities and innovative features, including a ballroom, Italianate roof garden, lounges, high-speed elevators, vacuum-type heating, one-hundred-car garage, and arcade of exclusive shops from which the co-owners would derive revenue to offset the maintenance cost of the unit. Luxurious furnishings were included in each unit, including Gorham silver, Bavarian china, and hand-tied Oriental rugs direct from the looms of the Far East. The Villa Riviera received National Register Historic status in 1996.

Throughout the 1920s, Lionel was one of the best-known real estate developers on the West Coast and the renowned expert in own-your-own development. He was a millionaire by the time he was twenty-four and a multimillionaire by age thirty-two. He had succeeded in his own right, but at home, things were falling apart.

The more successful Arthur Mayell became in oil drilling and church-board leadership, and the more Una traveled to speak, write, and teach Bible studies, the more estranged from one another they became. Lionel's mother was granted a divorce in 1924 on the grounds of alleged cruelty by his father and allegations that he had circulated false stories about her for defrauding him and using improper language. Lionel's father died the next year, and never lived to see his son's finest accomplishment, the Villa Riviera.

Lionel was rich, handsome, and successful, but he had no one to share his life with and he wasn't yet a Christian. It was the perfect combination to bring about his first failure.

It's amazing to think that my dad experienced so much success in building and commercial development, when he had no prior business or construction experience and no knowledge in buying materials, sales, or advertising. During his academic studies, he completed only one elective architectural design class at UCLA prior to transferring to Stanford.

Some might attribute his success to being at the right place at the right time. Others might wonder why God would bless a nonbeliever. But the Bible never says that blessings are reserved only for believers. Dad chose to honor God in the only way he knew at the time. He meditated on and believed Hebrews 11:6, that God existed and would reward him as he diligently sought Him. God tells us throughout Scripture that He honors His Word and that He puts His Word over His name (Isaiah 40:8; Psalms 138:2; and Jeremiah 1:12). In Isaiah 55:11, He reminds us:

> So will My word be which goes out of My mouth;
> It will not return to Me void (useless, without result),
> Without accomplishing what I desire,
> And without succeeding in the matter for which I
> sent it. (AMP)

Dad on spring break from Stanford, 1919, and the family Packard.

Cooper Arms, Long Beach, CA

Artaban, Long Beach, CA

Dad receiving award for Villa Riviera, Long Beach, CA

Villa Riviera, Long Beach, CA

ALL THAT GLITTERS

PEOPLE LINED UP AROUND the block of the 5,300-seat Angelus Temple, waiting to hear evangelical sensation Aimee Semple McPherson. "Sister Aimee" was drawing crowds of more than fifteen thousand people per day, seven days a week. She was America's most famous preacher, and the Angelus Temple was highly promoted by the city of Los Angeles as a tourist destination. It was the place to be in the early 1920s, and Lionel Mayell often attended to witness Sister Aimee's famous dramatic productions, called "illustrated sermons," and to hear his friend David Hutton sing in the choir.

Unlike that of other evangelical preachers of the day, the message given by Sister Aimee emphasized hope and love rather than hell and damnation, and her charismatic appeal cut across all denominations and walks of life. She was even approved by the Methodist church and other mainstream denominations.

David Hutton, an outstanding baritone and soloist at Angelus Temple, invited Lionel to attend a Methodist banquet with him one fall evening. There, he introduced Lionel to a beautiful young coloratura soprano who also sang in the three-hundred-plus-member choir, Marjorie Doolittle.

Marjorie's family had relocated to Los Angeles from Colorado so she could further her studies under well-known opera teacher and dramatic soprano Gloria Mayne-Windsor. Marjorie's mother worked at the upscale Buffum's Department Store in Long Beach. Lionel assumed Marjorie must be a Christian. After all, she sang in the choir and was attending a Methodist banquet. He cut a handsome figure in his 1919 Packard, one of the few cars at the banquet and certainly the finest. He offered to give her a ride home afterward.

At nineteen, Marjorie was a flashing beauty, with dancing, mischievous eyes and black hair. Young women were just starting to mimic the more relaxed social styles and coquettish baby talk they had seen in Hollywood film stars, and from the passenger seat of the Packard, Marjorie leaned over and playfully poked her finger in the big dimple on Lionel's right cheek. "You're my daddy. Can mama have that dimple?" she said in her best flirtatious talk. "Can that be mama's dimple? Can I always say that's my dimple?"

Lionel was swept off his feet. He asked Marjorie out on a date the very next night. And the next. And the next after that. He was sure it was love. He had found someone to share his life with. Just six weeks later, shortly after he completed his first luxury high-rise project, the Artaban, they married in October of 1922, in a simple afternoon ceremony attended only by immediate family. Lionel's mother and father were not in favor of the marriage, but their advice fell on deaf ears.

The trouble started almost immediately after the vows were spoken. Lionel learned that Marjorie was a Christian Scientist, and although he wasn't yet a Christian himself, he knew enough to understand that there was something fundamentally anti-Christian about Christian Scientism. This became the source of intense arguments, one of which played out in dramatic fashion aboard their honeymoon cruise down the St. Lawrence River in Canada.

"Daddy sweetheart, what are those big buildings with the towers along the river?" she asked.

"That's a Catholic hospital, Marjorie," Lionel answered.

She didn't believe in sickness, death, evil, or sin, and thought he was just taunting her because her religion didn't believe in such things. She immediately made a scene amid all the people on the deck, tore down the stairs, and locked herself in their stateroom for six or seven hours, refusing to participate in meals or activities. Bitter arguments over religion became standard fare for the marriage.

They made their home in the Mayell family residence in Long Beach, along with Lionel's mother and father. Una never approved of Marjorie since she was from the "wrong side of the tracks." Marjorie didn't have the refined social manners of someone from Una's background, and when Lionel brought her to the country club, she embarrassed Una in front of her club friends by eating with her fingers. To save face, Lionel pretended that eating with your fingers was quite customary in Europe, and the country club ladies bought his explanation.

Around that same time, the Mayell home became a bit more crowded when Una obtained guardianship of a thirteen-year-old foster child who attended Sunday school at her church. Una was superintendent of Sunday school for the large First Brethren Church of Long Beach when a young member, Emille Lee Stewart, made an appointment to see her after class. Visibly upset about something, Emille Lee told Una that her current guardians, the Stewarts, were going to take her out of school, move to Mojave for an opportunity to open a gas station, and force her to work there. She confided that the Stewarts were cruel to her and that she could not stand living with them anymore.

Una believed her story, used her considerable influence and wealth to obtain legal guardianship of Emille Lee, and changed her name to Carma Emille Lee Mayell (after her deceased son, Carman).

Between arguments over religious differences with her husband and the tension of living with a disapproving mother-in-law, Marjorie soon filed for divorce. Lionel realized he was in love with love but not with Marjorie, and in June of 1924, he granted her a divorce. The marriage had lasted only eighteen months. He agreed to let her keep the $2,000 engagement ring he had bought for her but refused to pay her alimony.

Four months after Lionel's divorce, Una was granted a divorce from Lionel's father. The following year, 1925, Arthur died. Even with his home life dismantled, Lionel's business career soared throughout his late twenties, with the completion of the Cooper Arms and the Villa Riviera projects. The Mayell household consisted of just three people now—Una, Lionel, and Carma. Una doted on Carma, treating her as if she were her own daughter. As Carma grew into a refined young adult, Una made sure she got the finest Christian college education and training in opera.

As the 1920s came to a close and Lionel completed the Villa Riviera, he sensed a period coming that would be the most serious ever for the business world. Sure enough, the Great Depression came in like a black cloud. He knew he wouldn't be able to finance, build, or sell beautiful luxury apartment homes for some time.

With Lionel unable to build or develop new projects, Una believed it would be good for the three of them to ride out the Depression in Europe. In 1930, they set sail for London, England, on the world's largest ocean liner, the *RMS Majestic*. The ship was so large that when she first docked in New York, no pier there was long enough to take her; at 956 feet in length, 41 feet of her stern projected into the Hudson River. The *Majestic* was the flagship of the White Star Line, and at over 56,000 tons, she was the largest steamer in the world.[6]

It is not clear whether this was part of Una's plan for her son all along, but by the time the Mayells arrived in London five days later, it was agreed that a successful businessman like Lionel should be married. And Carma, now a beautiful, sophisticated, and properly cultured woman of twenty years, would be a fitting choice. Lionel had known Carma since she was thirteen, and had watched her grow into a fine young religious-educated woman. They never argued, and while he shared more friendship than romantic love with her, he reasoned that it might make a better foundation for a marriage.

The sheer romanticism of the transatlantic crossing on the finest luxury liner, the elegant and intimate Ritz-Carlton dining experiences, the orchestral entertainment aboard ship, and the subtle suggestions by his mother all coalesced to make the idea seem like the thing to do—especially in retrospect of the constant quarreling of his first marriage.

News of the wedding splashed over all the society pages back in Southern California, with one newspaper noting that friends would be surprised to learn of the marriage of Carma Emille Lee to Lionel Vincent Mayell. Indeed, Lionel himself may have been surprised. They were married at the historic old Marylebone Presbyterian Church in London on August 1, 1930. By this time, Carma was a well-known and talented singer in Long Beach, having performed a solo concert at the opening of the Villa Riviera in 1929.

Following their wedding, Lionel and Carma toured the continent in grand style for three and a half months, entertained by royalty, rulers, and Europe's business and social elite. They honeymooned in the seaside resort of Brighton and on the Isle of Wight and attended the yacht races where King George V and Queen Mary were present. In Rome, they were escorted about the Vatican and the royal palace, were entertained by the secretary to Benito Mussolini, and even toured the private office of "Il Duce" himself. They even stayed several days in San Sebastian at the summer home of the king of Spain.

In all, they covered over twenty-five thousand miles through nine countries in a sleek French-manufactured Delahaye automobile driven by an English-speaking chauffeur. Carma took advantage of the opportunity to study voice under the most prominent opera instructors on the continent. Lionel noted that in almost every city they visited, tall multi-storied cooperative apartment projects dotted the skyline and large billboards advertised living in luxury "the New York way." The Old-World elegance was unparalleled, but they were sold on the same ninety-nine-year-lease basis of New York co-ops, and the monthly rental rates were exorbitant.

Being a visionary and teeming with passion for his idea, he initiated appointments with developers across Europe and presented them with samples of his deed-based ownership plans, sales contracts, title insurance policies, marketing materials, and photographs of his successful projects in Southern California. He explained the differences and advantages of true ownership, in which the buyer had a warranty deed to his or her apartment as opposed to a ninety-nine-year lease in a stock cooperative.

"What you're doing isn't ownership," Lionel explained. "You're making people think they're buying an ownership and they're only getting a lease, and when the lease is ninety-nine years old, it is canceled out, and the people and their heirs don't have anything."

The developers in Spain were immediately sold on the idea, and enthusiastically proposed that Lionel return to California to put his business in order, then come back to help them convert their projects across Spain to his concept of ownership. They offered to contract with him on any reasonable basis he suggested, even entering into a partnership with Mayell Enterprises for the rights to use his deed-based plan of apartment home ownership in Spain.

But Lionel was headstrong. He determined to go his own way, even amid the Great Depression. Not even his mother could change his mind. When he left Spain, he thought very little about the offer from the developers there, and it wasn't until years later that he realized what a significant opportunity he missed. He was still young and impetuous, and never thought about licensing or obtaining intellectual property protection for his unique deed-ownership model.

When he returned to Spain in the 1940s, Lionel Mayell's deed plan had been widely adopted throughout Europe.

————

Dad was high off his success as a builder, fresh into a second marriage, and enjoying a glamorous trip around Europe in the company of kings and queens. Notwithstanding that the world was spiraling into a severe economic depression, life for the Mayells went on much in the same lavish style they had been accustomed to, at least initially. Even so, the loss of a sense of purpose and the desire to live up to his mother's expectations for a proper marriage may have fueled a restlessness in my dad. He seemed to have no clear vision for where to take his life next, and he walked away from the one thing that had made him successful—his reliance on "diligently seeking" God.

THE GREATEST
SHOWMAN ON EARTH

L IONEL, CARMA, AND UNA Mayell returned home after
their three-and-a-half-month trip to Europe to find Southern
California suffering from the full force of the Great Depression,
much like the rest of the country. Businesses failed, workers lost
their jobs, and families fell into poverty. Banks throughout the
nation closed their doors, and thousands of individual investors
and depositors lost everything.

Although Lionel had money tied up in a bank and could not
build apartments, he still had the millions he made during the
previous decade. Unlike most citizens in the United States, he
did not have to work. Two years into their marriage, he and
Carma welcomed the first of two children, Lionel Vincent Jr.,
born in 1932. In 1934, daughter Myrna Yvonne was born.

Lionel had been working fifteen-hour days for as long as he
could remember, so he found it difficult to stay idle while waiting

for the Depression to lift. Even though he had a wife and two small children, he became restless and bored. He was ready for a new challenge.

One day, upon returning home from errands, he was greeted in the foyer of their Long Beach home by his mother. "Is it you, dear?" Before he could answer, she continued, "George Isaacs has been calling you all day. He's the son of your late father's tailor in London, Ontario. Be careful, son. I don't like the sound in his voice."

Lionel ignored his mother. He had met George several times and was impressed. He was a sharp guy and a go-getter. Over the years he had been the global executive secretary of the Imperial Conference of the Shriners, and he had successfully programmed great electrical pageants in Minneapolis and Los Angeles. At annual executive conferences, George was the brains behind great electrical pageantry parades down the cities' main streets at night, which had raised hundreds of thousands of dollars for the Shriners Hospitals in Minneapolis and LA.

Lionel went right to his private study and dialed George.

"Lionel, as you know, the Shriners have made tons of money through the electrical extravaganza," George told him. "I can sell you the electrical pageant for little money, and you could start promoting it as a great show-business tool for Hollywood and bring entertainment to America in a time when they desperately need distractions from the Depression."

Lionel was immediately hooked. They began to brainstorm.

"George, how about we hold talent contests all over the United States in the large sport stadiums and invite all the major players of Hollywood to sign contracts, while at the same time bringing an evening of fun to the packed arenas?"

"You could find new talent and make a huge name for yourself," George agreed.

Lionel signed the deal without any further thought. This vision could utilize his promotional skills, provide an escape for Americans, and give Hollywood new talent. But most of all, it would feed his need to be active. Although in every business endeavor up to that time he would pray, this time he did not. Not only did he not pray, but he also dipped into the money he had reserved for his tithe.

He did not know any of the major players in Hollywood, but Lionel began knocking on doors to all the studios, from MGM to Paramount, to introduce his idea. If the idea worked, the studios would benefit, everybody would win, and Lionel would make money.

After months of planning and relationship-building, he was ready to take the extravaganza on the road. He had redesigned the former Shriner floats into fourteen moveable stages that could carry hundreds of people, orchestras, and band equipment. From his own money, he paid Hollywood studios tens of thousands of dollars to reconfigure the floats according to his vision.

Each night's performance cost $25,000 to put on, but Lionel was a multimillionaire and brimming with confidence in his abilities. Each stage was pulled by a tractor-trailer, and the whole extravaganza was transported by fourteen freight cars and towed down the Mississippi River by tugboats on flatbed boats. They were illuminated with five hundred storage batteries beneath each float. Giant flowers made from colored foil and special material adorned each stage, and twenty-foot towers affixed to each float featured tiered platforms staged with beautiful women who were talent-show winners from nearby states.

To attract large crowds needed to fill the stadiums and arenas, Lionel negotiated with the who's-whos of Hollywood to make guest appearances. He built relationships with Hollywood stars and contracted with Ginger Rogers, Jean Harlow, Robert Taylor, and others to be the drawing cards for the crowds. In return, he paid them $5,000 to $7,000 per appearance, plus the cost for their sequined costumes and tuxes. He soon had the reputation of being able to pick out the right girls.

In addition to guest appearances, he held multiple talent shows in the surrounding cities prior to the big event, and gave many celebrities their start by connecting them to movie producers in Hollywood. Each night of the performance, fourteen moving stages showcased several hundred beautiful women in dazzling costumes that Lionel Mayell had designed and funded at a cost of several thousand dollars per city, per show. He contracted with Rudy Vallee, Ethel Merman, and Buddy Rogers to sing with their orchestras, which were set on the stages as the backdrop to the hundreds of showgirls.

His first show stop was the famous Cotton Carnival in Memphis, Tennessee. America was hungry for anything that would get their minds off the Depression. The excitement brought large crowds to opening night. The crowd was loud and so frenetic that thousands broke through the fence around the stadium and didn't pay admission. The first show had a loss of over $25,000.

Even so, Lionel refused to go home or give up. The next stop was Soldier Field in Chicago. The bleachers were full, with almost 50,000 people who paid $2 to $4 per person. The great floats with the orchestras and pretty girls and thousands of lights were slowly driven into the stadium by tractor trailers. The crowds roared with excitement, and Lionel loved it. The event closed with spectacular fireworks, and while the crowd focused on the fireworks, the center stage in the middle of the field was converted to a dance floor. At the end of the evening, hundreds of couples danced for hours while a big band orchestra played.

From Soldier Field, the show traveled to other cities, with the last show at the Cotton Bowl in Dallas, Texas. This extravaganza took about a year of planning and rescheduling due to many nights being rained out. Governor Jim Allred presented Lionel with a hand-engraved plaque that declared, "Lionel Mayell, The Greatest Showman on Earth." In his presentation, the governor said, "This show not only provided entertainment, great talent, and Hollywood greats, but provided a night of dancing with the greatest orchestras and bands of the day."

Lionel was done. He had fed his ego with the packed stadiums and the oohs and ahhs of the crowds. Across America, the show was reported as one of the most sensational in the United States. Still, the losses due to rain in Dallas made it a financial disaster. Because the shows occurred prior to the use of indoor stadiums, rainouts were frequent, but not sufficient to recover insurance money to offset the costs.

He used his own money to fix what the rain had damaged and went to the next city, hoping for a different outcome. In addition, people were desperate for entertainment but didn't have the money to buy tickets, so they broke through fences to see the show without paying. Hollywood celebrities demanded higher fees and more expensive costumes. Show after show chiseled away at his millions of dollars.

After being in Dallas for about a year and having been rained out repeatedly, Lionel's money was all spent. He had to go home, but he did not want to face his family as a failure. He had only enough money to pay for one-way bus fare to California, with not enough left over to buy even a sandwich or a cup of coffee.

Up to this time, everything he had touched turned to gold, but now it tarnished. In less than two years, the curtain went down on his great electrical extravaganza. On the long bus ride home, he rehearsed how he would spin the story of failure to his family.

Lionel had no idea what would greet him when he arrived home. His financial show-business failure was bad enough, but in his absence his entire family had been ripped apart. Carma had been left alone to raise their two children while living with his mother for almost two years. They had a roof over their heads, plenty of food, and financially had nothing to worry about, but she had not signed up for that kind of life.

While Lionel had traveled with the beautiful stars of Hollywood and gained the applause of people, she tired of being a single parent and under the scrutiny of her mother-in-law, who had first been her adopted mother. One day she decided to take the children and leave. The newspapers called it a kidnapping, but she was a woman who was heartbroken, tired, and angry. She probably did not know what else to do to gain her husband's attention.

Lionel was financially ruined and felt like a failure. Now he had no idea where his wife and children were. He hired a detective, filed for divorce, and gained custody of his children, which was unheard of for a man in 1936. But he had not won. He was a broken man full of regrets. He had not been a good husband or father, and had been too egotistical to care.

To add to his shame and remorse, Una reminded him that from the beginning she had said that his stint in show business would never succeed. After his divorce, she gave him a position managing one of the apartment buildings she owned in Los Angeles, sold their home in Long Beach, and moved to the corner of June Street and Wilshire Boulevard in the famous Hancock Park area of Los Angeles.

Her actions only fueled his feelings of inadequacy.

———

For years Dad carried regret over the decision of going into show business to feed his need for activity. Carelessly, he lost his fortune and family. His show-biz career was short lived but carried the lesson of a lifetime. Dad's ego had been fed and he began to believe that he no longer needed God as he had while building cooperative apartments. In fact, he said in a testimony, "I became my own God. And without even realizing what was happening, I was caught up in working alongside some of the greatest actors and actresses of the '20s and '30s, the famous movie studios, and only remembering the crowds cheering and stomping their feet in excitement." Instead of seeking and believing God, as he had learned through the life of John Wanamaker based on the promise in Hebrews 11:6, he only prayed for God to stop the rain and make him a big success.

Dad was not a Christian, but God was still working and He used this experience to build inside of him a sensitivity toward others who had experienced failure in business and family.

Some might say this was a detour, but God's plan is His plan. Although the Enemy is continuously undermining that plan, God uses every diversion or tactic of the Enemy and transforms it for our best. Dad used to say, "Nothing, nothing can separate us from the love of God. No mistake, no failure, no attitude. God will take anything and use it to develop our relationship with Him, establishing a greater trust and dependency." Often, our times of darkness can be God's tool to move us into what our Daddy God has always carried for us in His heart. God's love is always working, moving us on track and on purpose. That is what I call superabundant grace.

Years later, Dad's time in show business would affect our relationship, as illustrated in this story:

"It's not fair. I hate this house. I can't do anything around here. All my friends can go to movies, but not me," I told my parents. "I have to sit around at home, bored. Bored, I tell you. That's exactly what I am. Bored!"

"Lionel, just let her go to the movies this time," Mom suggested. "At least we won't have to hear her complaining."

"Dorothy, you know the reason I don't approve of our children going to the movies." Dad shook his head. "It isn't that I want our children to be left out and not have fun. But if we let Ritalynn go this time, we've let down our standards, and it will be easier for her to go the next time and the next. Why can't she be content like her brother and sister?"

Mom sighed. "Okay. But I think you better explain to her why she can't go. She's different, you know. She likes to know why."

When Dad approached me, I spoke loudly to get my point across. "San Bernardino is boring, and all of my Christian friends are able to go to the movies, and their parents are on staff with Campus Crusade and they love the Lord. So don't tell me going to the movies isn't Christian. Just don't go down that road." I was rude and, quite frankly, hateful. At age fourteen, I believed I was mature enough to make my own decisions.

"You do know what boredom leads to, right?" I threatened. "I guess I'll just have to party. The churches we go to are over eighty miles one way because of support-raising, so I don't have any local activities. I live in a prison!"

It was Dad's gaze—his soft-blue dancing eyes—that melted my heart. It was as if he knew what I was thinking when he began to speak. "Ritalynn, your daddy used to get bored and restless too. I always wanted to be out doing something. I couldn't just be still. My mind was constantly racing and thinking of new things to do. In those early days, I had religion—a lot of head knowledge—without relationship with Jesus, so I didn't know how to hear God and learn what my boredom was all about. So if something was presented that sounded like it would use my gifts and make money, I jumped at the opportunity. Unfortunately, I jumped without considering how it would impact anyone else, including my wife and children. I was selfish and all about me, and today I still carry the heartache of that choice in the lives of my older children, Vince and Myrna. I don't want you to make the same mistakes I made because you're bored. Boredom can lead you down a lot of wrong paths. It did for me, and Ritalynn, you're a lot like me."

For a long time, I never understood about not going to movies. It took years to sort through the legalism and misunderstanding, and to realize that it was never about the movies; it was about my heart, and the motive behind my needing to be active. Dad tried to share his firsthand knowledge of the bitterness and emptiness he had experienced in Hollywood, and he did not want me to idolize another's life. For him, movies represented too much of this painful time in his life. The lesson in this story was not about Hollywood or acting; it was about a life without Christ.

Our Daddy God is always faithful to take the infallible seeds of another and water them with truth and grace. Dad had to learn that nothing in the outside world would ever fulfill the emptiness of his heart apart from a personal relationship with Jesus Christ. God used Dad's experience in the entertainment industry to ultimately bring Dad into relationship with Him. And like Dad, I too had my own journey to walk, and my own encounter with the Savior to experience.

CHAPTER SIX

RATIONING AND ROMANCE

T IMING IS EVERYTHING—OR, MORE accurately, God's timing is everything. Often, it is during the experiences we see no purpose for, that we discover an overarching hand guiding us into an amazing destiny way beyond our dreams. First Corinthians 2:9 tells us, "'No eye has seen, no ear has heard, no heart has imagined, what God has prepared for those who love Him'" (BSB).

During the height of his career as a developer in the 1920s, before the Depression and his stint in show business, Lionel had purchased five hundred acres of desert land near Palm Springs and the main highway, along the old Route 26 (now Interstate 10) between Indio and Los Angeles. He had never made that kind of land purchase before.

"What were you thinking, son?" Una had asked at the time, with an edge of condescension. "That land is a waste of good money, and once again you've made a poor business decision."

Lionel didn't have a good answer. He did not know why. His mother was right on some level. It did appear to be a poor business decision. He could not build on the land because every other section surrounding his parcel was American Indian land and they would not allow commercialization. The only way to develop anything on his land would be to violate and trespass on their territory.

Now having lost his fortune in show business and feeling like a failure, he turned his attention to the only thing he still owned: the seemingly useless parcel of land near Palm Springs. To find a solution, he went directly to the Indians' real estate agent to work out a deal, but he could not convince them. He was never one to give up easily, though, so he researched and contacted every land owner within eight miles to discuss options. Time and again, he met only problems, not solutions.

Lionel had walked away from God while he was in show business, but now he recalled how God had been faithful to reward him in his business. The promise of Hebrews 11:6, that God "is a rewarder of those who diligently seek him" again offered hope. Humbled, he prayed and believed God for a solution.

He mapped out all the possibilities and stepped out in faith in the direction that brought him peace. After praying, his friend Alphonzo Bell Jr. came to mind. Alphonzo was a descendant of the pioneering ranching, oil, and real estate development family that gave its name to the Southern California communities of Bell, Bell Gardens, and Bel Air, and developed the communities of Westwood, Beverly Hills, Pacific Palisades, and Bel Air. Lionel shared his idea with Alphonzo, an executive in his father's oil business, and Alphonzo offered to loan him his large 90L tractor and introduce him to oil companies that could potentially sell him discarded waste oil.

It appeared that Lionel was on his way to successfully connecting a road that would ensure development of his land. But the city of Palm Springs was against having a shorter route from the state highway and the railroad tracks because they thought it would invite hobos and crime into their city. Even so, Lionel was a convincing orator, and he won over their dispute and received permission to shorten the way into Palm Springs.

Excited about the new road and development potential in the desert, Alphonzo volunteered the use of his corporate attorneys, who discovered a loophole in the regulations that gave Lionel permission from the Federal Government to build a road over the sections of Indian land without trespassing their rights.

Lionel surveyed his five hundred acres of desert property and surrounding land, borrowed the trucks from Alphonzo, and contracted with several major oil companies (including Alphonzo's) for their discarded non-usable oil. Since the big heavy oil trucks could not navigate over the desert sand, he used Alphonzo's tractors with extra-large tires capable of pulling the great oil tankers across the desert while spraying hot oil over the contoured surfaces he had designed and carefully mapped out on paper.

As the hot oil covered the desert, Lionel followed on foot to personally ensure that the oil truck sprayers did not get clogged and leave a spot uncovered. He had also arranged for dozens of friends to partially deflate their car tires and slowly drive across the top of the oiled surface to pat it down. The last challenge of the project was that Lionel had never obtained permission to oil over the railroad tracks, so he sprayed up to the edge and placed old railroad ties between the tracks to create a smooth driving surface, completing the desert highway into Palm Springs.

That paved road in the desert is known today as Ramon Road, one of the main roads that connect Thousand Pines directly to Palm Springs. This entire project began as a way for Lionel to gain access to his five hundred acres of land, for which he had paid $1 an acre. Now with an access road, the land greatly increased in value.

Less than one month later, he traded this land for a $150,000 apartment building in Los Angeles, which he gave to his mother for reasons unknown and for which she assumed a small mortgage. Maybe the land wasn't such a bad investment for $500 after all. Maybe it was just a stepping stone so they could acquire a much more valuable piece of real estate. Or was it?

As 1937 dawned, Lionel thought that surely the Depression would lift and the economy would recover. Then he could start building apartments again. Faint signs of recovery appeared, enough to give the country a taste of optimism. Employment picked up and spending looked promising. The Golden Gate Bridge opened, a new commercial flight record from Los Angeles to New York was achieved, and the United Auto Workers Union promised better wages and hours.

Then several tragic events again battered a fledgling economy: a major flood along the Mississippi and Ohio Rivers caused millions to lose their homes, the Hindenburg exploded, and Amelia Earhart disappeared on an around-the-world journey. The nation's optimism again sank into deep pessimism, and 1937 ushered in another recession, the third worst in the twentieth century. The private sector construction industry was impacted the most, followed by a downturn in heavy industry and the manufacturing of durable goods. Lionel could not move. He was forced to stay right where he was.

In a recorded speaking engagement years later, Lionel described this time of his life, "I had been stripped of everything I had used to prove to myself that I was valuable. It was all gone in six years. I felt like my life was over. I had lost my business profit, been divorced twice, and was living under my mother's roof to be constantly reminded that I was a no-good runt and failure. The only thing that kept me going were my two children."

Lionel Mayell, the pioneer builder, multimillionaire visionary whose buildings dotted the Long Beach landscape, who had honeymooned throughout Europe at the peak of the Great Depression, who had lavishly spent his millions in show business, was still financially broke. To add to the humiliation, he was forced to work for his mother managing the very apartment building that he had traded for his land in Palm Springs.

The one possession he still had from his first fortune was his V-12, dual-ignition Pierce Arrow, which he had custom built to be two inches longer and sport the largest engine of any Pierce Arrow in the world. At the time, it cost $11,000, and the sales literature referred to the engine as the "Greatest of All Twelves."

The apartment building was occupied mostly by elderly widowed women, and as part of his management responsibilities, Lionel was their driver for errands. Reflecting back on this, he said, "It was the worst time of my life. I was working long hours while managing my mother's apartment building and driving the elderly boarders on errands. I could not find God anywhere and assumed that He, too, had abandoned me. I believed that all I was ever going to do was cater to the elderly renters in my mother's apartment building."

But God had never left Lionel, and His plan from the beginning was still on track and on time. Lionel was still not a Christian, only a social church-goer, but God had never stopped wooing him. At the time, he could not possibly imagine that this job was a blessing, but later he would recognize the fingerprint of God.

One spring day, Lionel was deeply absorbed in the morning's routine at Hawarden Hall Apartments in Long Beach, when a radiant young woman about nineteen years of age walked in with her mother to look at one of the apartments. She had the deepest blue eyes and big dimples, and her personality was effervescent. Her name was Dorothy Anderson, named after her mother. Lionel took his time showing them the apartment and every detail that might prove to be the one point that would seal the deal.

An hour later, they walked out without committing, but Lionel knew in his heart they would return. There was something different about Dorothy Anderson. He later said he knew the moment she walked in that day that she would become his wife. Years later Dorothy would confirm, "Lionel's apartment was not the best one we had seen that day, but both Mother and I felt that we needed to rent that one." A few days later, the Andersons became tenants.

Dorothy and her mother had moved to California from Ogden, Utah, to find better weather conditions for Dorothy's mother. The harsh Utah winters had wreaked havoc on her health, and her doctor recommended the sunny, temperate, dry climate of Southern California. Dorothy's father was a railroad conductor, and with the Great Depression in full force, he could not afford to give up his good-paying job and stayed behind in Ogden. Sadly, Dorothy would see her father only one more time.

Lionel felt protective of the Andersons, and provided extra attention to ensure they had everything they needed. He singled out Dorothy and often asked if she needed anything from the store as an excuse to get her to join him for a ride in the Pierce Arrow. He beamed when Dorothy accepted and jumped into the car right next to him, but their time alone lasted only momentarily. The sound of the dual engine of the Pierce Arrow alerted all the elderly boarders, and in perfect unison they yelled sweetly from above, "Baby, where are you going?"

"Oh, just down the street to the store," came the reply.

"Oh, good. We will be right down."

Within minutes, a carload of boarders descended on the Pierce Arrow with their bags and sun parasols, crowding Dorothy out of the front seat and into the back. It was difficult for Lionel to have a conversation with her, as the boarders constantly interrupted with their own stories. Lionel accommodated their requests for multiple errands and destinations, but quickly realized they were just meddling because he had taken a special interest in Dorothy.

He tried to avoid their prying eyes and spend some precious time alone with Dorothy. He planned weekend outings for just the two of them—a picnic, a day of shopping, or a visit to the beautiful city of Pasadena. Nothing worked. Each time the boarders heard the Pierce Arrow, they raised the upper windows, yelled down for Lionel to hold the car, and joined in for wherever they happened to be going. If they sensed even the slightest hesitation on Lionel's part, they reminded him of his obligation to drive them and even threatened to complain to his mother. He resented their intrusion, but the pattern continued for six long years of their courtship.

Lionel knew he had to find a way to gain independence, but with the country in a recession, jobs were scarce. The Los Angeles area was home to six of the country's major aircraft manufacturers, and although the United States had not yet entered World War II, conflicts were building in other parts of the world.

In 1936–1937, the U.S. military awarded a contract for production of several hundred B-18 Bombers to Douglas Aircraft in Santa Monica. Lionel seized the opportunity. He went to the Douglas Aircraft headquarters and got hired on the spot, making 55 cents per hour. It wasn't what he had been accustomed to, but he felt fortunate to have a job. Dorothy, unbeknownst to Lionel at the time, had also been hired by Douglas for 57 cents per hour.

When the United States entered World War II in 1942, the government instituted a policy of rationing gas and even some food items and clothing. This meant sacrifices for almost everyone, but those whose work was deemed essential to the war effort were classified differently. Because of Lionel's job at Douglas Aircraft, he was issued unlimited coupons for gas and additional stamps for food and clothing. He was able to use the large Pierce Arrow to transport other employees to work at Douglas, and for errands on behalf of the apartment building. Lionel saved his extra coupons for special weekend outings with Dorothy.

Although the country was mobilizing its energies toward supporting the war effort, the effects of the Great Depression lingered on, and millions of people still struggled to find work. A gallon of gas was 19 cents in 1941,[7] and the average cost of a new car was only $850, but the average worker made only $1,750 per year in wages. Not many families could afford the cost of a new home at $4,075.[8]

Like Lionel, Dorothy Anderson also had an interesting background story. She had been raised as an only child who had been given everything her parents could offer—love, material gifts, and education—but her parents could not introduce her to Jesus Christ because they did not know Him personally. Her parents taught her a few Bible verses around Christmas and Easter, but that was it. Dorothy was an "A" student, active in many clubs, played a classical saxophone, and won many honors across the Rocky Mountain States. The day she and her mother turned around one block from Lionel's apartment, her life changed forever.

As Dorothy and Lionel spent more time together, she observed that he and his mother spoke frequently about Jesus Christ in a personal way. Having a personal relationship with Jesus was a new concept to her, but she concluded that she had to be "religious" to get into the Mayell family, so she developed a strategy to do just that.

She couldn't just talk to Lionel about it when they were alone because they were seldom alone. He had two young children, a mother who was always around, Dorothy's mother, and an apartment mostly filled with retired widows who thought of him as a son. Everywhere the couple went, at least two or three boarders or the children accompanied them. Instead, she asked if she could attend church downtown with Lionel and Una. The Mayells were thrilled, and Dorothy believed this would move their relationship in the right direction. And it did.

With her intelligence, Dorothy soon picked up some religious terminology and began to use the words in conversation even though she had no idea what they meant. When Lionel and Una joined the church, Dorothy felt left out. She had never heard of joining a church, but decided that this must be the thing to do to become a worthy bride to a Mayell. Years later she said in her testimony, "I had to do everything for the man I loved, and it was critical to gain his mother's approval."

Dorothy learned that to become a member, she had to be "interviewed." She had no idea what that interview would entail, but she had a plan for finding out. For several consecutive Sundays, she inconspicuously followed every prospective member down to the front of the church and sat right behind them in the second row, close enough to hear what was being said. She made notes on every question, every answer, and the corresponding Bible verses. She then went home and memorized the answers she had heard along with the Scripture verses. She successfully joined the church and became a very devoted member of the Church of the Open Door, one of the largest evangelical churches in the country.

Dorothy became the consummate Christian actress. She did not have the satisfaction of the one thing she was seeking—a personal relationship with Christ—and neither did Lionel, for almost another eight years.

———

One of my most favorite stories shared by Mom and Dad reveals the hand of God in directing our decisions and plans—even what we consider mistakes—and integrating them into our destiny:

When Dad purchased the five hundred acres of land in Palm Springs, it was at least a decade before he met Mom. The investment didn't make any sense because it had limited development value. But building the access road allowed him to trade the five hundred acres for a much more valuable apartment building in Long Beach. And that apartment building was the place Mom chose, out of all the other apartments they visited in Southern California, because she felt drawn to it.

Often, what we perceive as a waste or happenchance, is a thread being woven by our heavenly Father into an amazing tapestry that He had planned from the beginning of time. We cannot fail or lose with Him. He is a rewarder to those who believe He is, and He searches for us far more intensely than we search for Him.

COULD THIS BE MY LIFE?

L IONEL HAD BEEN DATING Dorothy Anderson for close to four years, with both of them continuing to work at Douglas Aircraft. He lived in his mother's beautiful home while Dorothy and her mother moved to an apartment in Los Angeles to be closer to the Mayells.

No longer responsible for managing the Long Beach apartment house or driving the tenants on errands, he took Dorothy on longer trips, but new circumstances prevented their being entirely alone. The Pierce Arrow was a prestigious automobile, and very few people knew how to work on them. As a bit of insurance against mechanical problems, Lionel persuaded his mechanic to bring his girlfriend along on their weekend drives to Palm Springs. He even purchased spare parts in advance and stored them in the third seat.

Palm Springs was a 180-mile round trip from Los Angeles, and it was Lionel's favorite place to take Dorothy—romantic with majestic mountain views and palm-tree-lined streets and twinkling streetlights. Its restaurants and one-of-a-kind shops were tastefully manicured with desert flowers, earning it the reputation as the winter playground for Hollywood, European royalty, and the wealthy. Una was right there among all the celebrities, having purchased a sprawling second home in the Merito Vista subdivision on the south side of Via Lola, during a time when so many Americans were losing their only home.

For Lionel, who made only 55 cents an hour at Douglas Aircraft, taking Dorothy to Palm Springs in a car that only got four miles to the gallon was a big investment. It required forty-five gallons of gasoline to make the trip, and at 19 cents a gallon, that was the equivalent of two days' wages. He also had to pay for two parking spaces because the eleven-passenger Pierce Arrow was so large and wide that it would not fit into one space.

But even with all the economic uncertainty of the Depression and the war, Lionel was sure of one thing: he wanted to marry Dorothy. She was different from Marjorie or Carma. Both his friend and his partner, she listened to and encouraged him in his ideas and was willing to play an active part in everything he desired to do. He had never experienced a partner who truly stood beside him. He adored and respected Dorothy, and valued her input. The respect she received from Lionel filled the gap she felt from not having a father who could affirm her value, worth, confidence, and purpose. They had a deep love for one another, and there was only one barrier: Lionel's mother.

Una never accepted Dorothy and did everything she could to hinder their relationship. She even threatened to change her will. On the long drives to Palm Springs, Lionel spent the time hoping and praying that each trip would be the one that changed his mother's mind about the woman he loved. That day never came. But Lionel noticed the change that was taking place inside him. He became unfazed by Una's threats to cut him off financially. He was willing to risk it all for the love of his life.

In faith, and without his mother's blessing, he proposed to Dorothy on Christmas Day in 1941, in the picturesque city of Palm Springs. Dorothy was not expecting a ring without Una's approval, and Lionel wanted to surprise her. With a twinkle in his eyes, he carried from his mother's guest bedroom a large suit box he had hidden away. It had been meticulously wrapped by Lionel himself, a talent which Dorothy would soon discover about her fiancé.

Inside the suit box was a smaller box, just as beautifully wrapped. And inside that box was another, and another, and another, each successively smaller until the smallest box was revealed—a tiny exquisitely wrapped ring box. With tears in his eyes, he kneeled in front of her and pledged his love and commitment to her. Una was close by in her master bedroom, close enough to hear, but she never joined them.

In a letter to Dorothy dated the spring of 1942, Lionel wrote, "It is with the greatest joy and delight to know that you will be mine forever, and I yours. I have never known this kind of love and joy existed. My Dorothy darling, I am saddened by my mother's inability to see what I have always seen in you. Instead, she has allowed one's heritage as a determination of their worth."

For two years following their engagement, Lionel faithfully arranged for Dorothy to spend time with his mother, hoping that her eyes would be opened. They never were. In February of 1943, Una passed away and was buried in her private garden with its locked key entrance at the famous Forest Lawn cemetery in Glendale, California. (Forest Lawn has been humorously referred to as "Disneyland for the dead." Appropriate then that Walt Disney ended up there.) Lionel buried his mother, although it was not the celebration he had hoped for. He laid his mother in the Mayell plot, and over the years frequented her garden as he shared with his family the power of forgiveness.

Two weeks after her death, the executor of Una's estate announced that she had indeed cut Lionel, her only child, out of her will and left her entire estate to his children, Vince and Myrna. Even her two homes, while in Lionel's name legally, carried the stipulation that they were only for the benefit of his children. As heartbreaking as this was, Lionel loved his mother and refused to ever say one unkind thing about her. He was now free to marry the love of his life, and four months later he did just that.

On the afternoon of November 26, 1943, two hundred and fifty guests were escorted through the grand marble foyer and the double French doors into the gardens of 684 South June Street in Hancock Park. Four dozen floral masterpieces adorned the altar and three seven-foot patio fountains created a calm ambience, while guests milled around the grand piano and hors d'oeuvres tables decorated with white linen tablecloths and white lilies, orchids, and assorted roses. The wedding of Lionel Mayell and Dorothy Anderson was the wedding of the year, announced in all the society sections of the Los Angeles, Hollywood, and Long Beach newspapers.

Dorothy wrote in her wedding memoirs, "Twenty minutes prior to the wedding, my hair was still in curlers, my mother and I were finishing up plating the rest of the hors d'oeuvres and food, and Lionel was scraping off the remaining paint from underneath his fingernails from a last-minute touch-up job. Vince was running in the back door with the huge wedding cake with Myrna behind him, making sure nothing would fall, as the guests streamed in through the gardens. They had no clue what was going on inside the back section of the mansion."

This kind of excitement and last-minute rush would become a way of life for Lionel and Dorothy—the two of them scurrying around together, preparing food for a celebratory dinner that they were hosting. They were indeed partners for life, having fun with the other. Their love was contagious, and their home was the place people wanted to come.

The wedding was officiated by Louis Talbot, pastor of the Church of the Open Door and the president of Biola and founder of Talbot Seminary. Many well-known Christians attended, including Henrietta Mears, a Christian educator, evangelist, and author who greatly impacted evangelical Christianity in the twentieth century, and his Occidental college roommate, Louis Evans Sr., who was pastor of the First Presbyterian Church of Hollywood. Still, despite all these connections, neither Dorothy nor Lionel had a personal relationship with Jesus Christ.

As the bridal march sounded, Dorothy walked down the aisle carrying a large bouquet of white roses and white orchids. From the beginning, Lionel had called her his White Rosebud. He often told her he saw her as a pure and wholesome gift, full of quiet beauty and one to be remembered in reverence. Traditionally, white roses are associated with marriages and new beginnings. But neither she nor Lionel could foresee how many new beginnings were just around the corner.

Their honeymoon was untraditional as well. Dorothy wrote of it, "We began our wedding journey with Lionel, his two children, and my mother piled into the Pierce Arrow. We stopped about 7 p.m. for the opening of the Derby House in Colton, where Lionel had arranged for special music to be played in honor of our marriage. We proceeded to Palm Springs, dropping off the children and Mother at the Del Tahquitz Hotel, and Lionel and I proceeded to the very private and romantic beautiful guest house at the estate of a friend. Our house was beautifully surrounded by date palms, scarlet hibiscus, and flowering jasmine. Every morning Lionel would bring me fresh squeezed orange juice from the citrus trees and would sit down and gaze into my eyes and tell me how much he adored me. Could this be really my life?"

———

Years later, Dad shared in a testimony that from the beginning of their relationship, Mom had made it easy for him to love, and she was used to bring healing to his own wounded heart. He said, "Dorothy was the one who told me that Vince and Myrna could not be left alone. That they needed their father and could not feel abandoned." She suggested that her mother come along on their honeymoon to take care of the children while she and Dad spent time alone.

Dad was overwhelmed with her compassion and her heart, thinking of the needs of his children. That was Mom. Over the next thirty-five years, their love and admiration would exponentially grow and deepen into the most beautiful love relationship. God knew exactly what experiences would best cultivate their relationship into a partnership that would become one voice and one heart, for a purpose more magnificent than the other could possibly imagine.

Mom and Dad's wedding, Los Angeles, CA, 1943

Mom and Dad's Home on South June Street, Los Angeles, CA, 1943

PARTNERS IN TRAINING

I T IS NEVER EASY returning from a honeymoon to a routine
life, but Dorothy loved being wife to Lionel and stepmother
to Vince and Myrna. Besides, there was never anything routine
about being married to Lionel Mayell. He was full of ideas and
vision, and she knew from dating him for six years that it was
exactly what she desired.

The management at Douglas Aircraft saw Lionel's hard work
ethic and it paid off. He was promoted several times, finally
becoming a grave-shift supervisor over three departments,
making $4.80 per hour. They also sent him to UCLA to take
architectural and structural design classes. God would put that
same architectural design knowledge to use in Lionel's business
career in the years to come.

In the beginning, Lionel was concerned about working
the grave shift and how that might affect his relationship with
Dorothy. But she encouraged him to see it as an opportunity to
make more money. He said later in a recording that the word

opportunity jumped out at him and he kept it close to his heart. He wasn't yet at a place where he could know that when things "leapt" in his heart, it was how God spoke to him.

At work, Lionel observed excessive amounts of scrap metal being discarded. He determined there had to be another use for it. Americans who lived during the war became resourceful, and it was common for them to save items, especially anything metal, and find creative ways to reuse them. Times were tough, and people got tougher. They got by with less, and did more to help out. Lionel was no different.

He knew that even though he had been promoted four times at Douglas Aircraft, he was not going to be satisfied working in the aircraft industry long term. His passion was to create, design, build, and see the end result. Although America was at war and the Depression had not lifted from the construction industry, he searched for ways to use his motivational gifts and skills to build, sell, influence, and lead.

The Douglas Aircraft plant spread over several city blocks, being so large that it demanded mail delivery by people on roller skates. During his breaks at work, Lionel sketched an idea he had been thinking about for months, a way to reuse the scrap metal from airplane propellers that were being phased out and replaced by jet engines.

His idea was to salvage the scrap metal and transform it into a ride-on toy "coaster" or scooter for kids. He investigated what was involved in taking the scrap metal and shaping it into tops for racers, then got permission to use the tools at work and made a temporary prototype. It was about three feet long and eight inches high, with ball-bearing rollers on four wheels, lever-mounted hand brakes, and beautiful hand-painted designs on the body. He couldn't wait to take home his toy model and present it to Dorothy.

She immediately caught his vision and encouraged him to manufacture it. On weekends when he was not working, both he and Dorothy strategically mapped out a plan for production and promotion with the marketing edge that it was a toy produced from World War II planes.

Dorothy was a talented chef like her mother, and she loved to cook for as many guests as they could afford to have for dinner. Over the next several weeks, Lionel invited several supervisors at Douglas for one of her famous home-cooked meals. After the meal, he presented his idea of starting a toy-manufacturing business on the side and invited each guest to think about being a potential investor. His plan covered all the details, including the structure and operations of the business, the materials necessary for production, workers, advertising, and promotional campaigns. He had researched and knew the numbers he needed to launch his toy-manufacturing business, and before long he had the investors and the $150,000 capital he needed.

Lionel was now ready to take his vision from the think tank into production. He incorporated his toy business through the corporation department of California, rented a vacant plant, purchased necessary equipment, and began production of the toy coasters. Employees from Douglas who needed second jobs were recruited to work on their off hours. He obtained permission to take the leftover non-usable scrap metal from Douglas and convert it to "ash residue" used to make the tops of the coasters.

Everything was in place. Production started and he began to promote his scooters to the large department stores throughout Southern California. Everything was working flawlessly, but he had not anticipated the interest by the department stores in Chicago and New York City. For Christmas, everyone wanted a toy made from material used in the war. His scooters became that holiday season's big-ticket item from coast to coast.

From September through November, Lionel received orders from every major department store in America, totaling over $275,000 in sales. He and the investors were thrilled. The demand was so great, he was forced to acquire additional manufacturing space and hire more workers. Employees worked double shifts to build and store coasters for fulfillment of orders through Dunn & Bradstreet. Retailers demanded shipment of their coasters in time for Christmas, which meant a manufacturing turnaround of less than three months.

Lionel and Dorothy worked side by side, with her providing the encouragement and support he needed. They each worked full shifts at Douglas, then left to work several more hours in the toy factory. She took breaks to go home and cook meals for the children, then rejoined him to serve him dinner after the children were tucked in bed. But even with extra workers and double shifts, they still could not produce fast enough to meet the overwhelming demand. Most orders were never fulfilled, and many who had ordered skipped out on payment as soon as the Christmas season was over.

For the orders he could not fulfill, Lionel returned every dime paid in advance. When the books were balanced, he had just enough money to pay back each of the investors in the corporation. No profit was earned. The toy factory shut down, and Lionel sold his invention, without the protection of a patent, to a major toy company that later made millions on his idea.

Some may view the toy-manufacturing venture as a wasted experience or a failure. But God used this as preparation for His purposes and plans for Dad and Mom. He knew exactly what they needed to groom them for what He had planned.

In the Bible, David prepared for his confrontation with Goliath by killing a bear and then a lion. Mom and Dad's experience allowed them a preparatory drill that created a tighter partnership of working closely together. It built inside Dad a confidence and an awareness of his gifting, and an appreciation of the gift of Mom's support and many talents. He was further equipped with the skills to build a business on his own—an understanding of how to set up a corporation, hire workers, advertise, and promote a vision. God was in every detail. What appeared to be a waste was the love of a heavenly Father who used this experience as the tool that would leverage them toward their destiny and success.

God was in the seemingly insignificant details as well, such as the precise location of the manufacturing space Dad had rented. The toy company was right across the street from a candy company called Bright's California Confections, and the two young businessmen, Dad and Bill Bright, became close friends. Bill Bright would one day found Campus Crusade for Christ, and neither Bill nor Dad knew then that over the next forty years, they and their wives would serve side by side for the same purpose.

Scooter Prototypes, 1943

From Religion to Relationship

THE MAYELLS SETTLED INTO a less demanding life after the toy-manufacturing business, and turned their focus to raising their children, attending weekly church activities, and entertaining friends in their spacious Wilshire Boulevard home. They thought of themselves as good Christians, were happy in their marriage, and believed they possessed everything they needed to make a life together. They read the Bible, and even prayed together from time to time.

Then, after one of their dinner parties, their live-in house-keeper, Randy, asked Lionel a life-changing question: "Mr. Mayell, have you ever been born again?"

"Randy, how dare you ask me that," Lionel said. "You know we always have Christians over for dinner and attend church, and you see all the Bibles around the house." He would not discuss the matter further, but could not get the question out of his mind. The seed was planted.

Lionel began to question if he really had invited Christ into his heart. He recalled that his roommates in college constantly talked about a "new birth," but he assumed it was for others and not for himself. After all, he had grown up with Christian teachings, worked in Billy Sunday's campaign, entertained the most well-known Christian evangelists in their home, and had studied Greek for five years. Even so, he said nothing about his doubts to his wife Dorothy.

But something was stirring inside Dorothy's heart too. She had noticed that Vince and Myrna, now thirteen and eleven, were being influenced by Hollywood, and she was searching for something wholesome and fun that might capture their attention. As she sat down to read the newspaper one morning, an article caught her attention. It told of a dynamic Christian group geared toward teenagers, and, surprisingly, it met each Saturday night at their own church, the Church of the Open Door at Biola.

Dorothy wasn't sure how she was going to share this with Lionel. She knew he was concerned too, but she didn't want to burden him after a double shift at work. Just then, she heard the key in the back door. Before she could say a word, he told her, "I've been pondering something for a while and needed to share it with you. I'm greatly concerned over the children being in Hollywood so much of the time, and I just don't know what to do."

"Oh, Lionel, I've been concerned too and didn't want to worry you," she confessed. "I've been worrying about this for days, but guess what? Today when I just happened to be reading the paper, I found something interesting. There's a new meeting being started at our church called Youth for Christ. From what I read, there has been attendance of about three thousand young people around Vince and Myrna's age. The program includes music the children would like, and according to the newspaper, the speakers are funny and provide entertainment. This might be something we could try and see if it would keep them out of Hollywood. At least one night a week. We could take them this Saturday and drop them off. What do you think?"

He was elated. "This sounds too good to be true. But I'd like to make one suggestion. Rather than drop them off at the door, let us go with them and stay. If they're anything like their father, they'll run off as soon as we drop them off."

The matter was settled, and the following Saturday night the family set out for the Youth for Christ event at the Church of the Open Door. The church was packed, and Lionel circled the building desperately trying to find a parking place. Could all these people be here for the Youth for Christ meeting?

As they neared the entrance of the church, loud music and the voices of thousands of kids greeted them. Dorothy looked at Lionel. "Honey, are you sure we can stay? I mean, we'll be the oldest ones here. I don't want the kids to feel embarrassed."

He wanted to leave and go have a quiet dinner somewhere with her, but something beckoned him inside. He took her hand. "It'll be okay."

They had hoped to sit inconspicuously near the back of the auditorium, but a young usher escorted the Mayells all the way to the front and seated them in the third row. All four of them felt self-conscious. Vince and Myrna were a little embarrassed to be with their parents, and Lionel and Dorothy had just crashed a youth meeting.

Hearing such lively music in church was unusual. They were used to orchestra music, somber and stoic. But Dorothy loved it. It reminded her of the days when she traveled throughout the Rocky Mountain States, playing jazz saxophone. Even Lionel started tapping his foot. They glanced around. The kids there were actually having fun. They began to relax. One by one, kids got up and shared how they had asked Jesus Christ into their hearts and how different their lives had become.

As they listened to the testimonies of the young adults, Lionel and Dorothy soon lost their self-consciousness and tuned out everything but the speaker. For the first time, they heard the good news of the gospel explained in an individual, personal way: "God loves you and has a plan for your life. And because of God's personal love for you, He brought Jesus to bridge the gap between you and God, and He promises to give you an abundant life."

Could this really be true? Maybe these speakers were just young and off base.

Evangelist Bob Pierce then took the pulpit. "The gospel is the too-good-to-be-true news," he said. "This is what the Bible calls God's mercy, not giving us what we deserve, and grace— Jesus doing it all for us. Grace is God's gift, and it lasts forever."

Dorothy was not about to look at Lionel, and Lionel was not going to look at Dorothy. They could sense the stirring in their hearts. But what would people think if they acted like they did not know this basic truth? The Church of the Open Door was *their* church, and Lionel's mother had been a prominent member for years. The pastor, Louis Talbot, had performed their wedding vows, and he had interviewed Dorothy when she joined the church. What would *he* think? Not only that, but they had hosted all the kids' parents in their home and had prayed so eloquently over their meals.

That night on the ride home, they avoided any discussion about it. When they stopped for ice cream, the kids chattered about the service and clearly wanted to return the following week. Lionel announced that next week they would just drop them off at the door. Although neither he nor Dorothy was willing to say it, they could not stop thinking about the message they had just heard.

The following week, when the time came to take the children to the Youth for Christ meeting, Lionel said, "Dorothy darling, I know this is last minute, but I think we need to go again to make sure the kids don't leave. I don't want them to miss out, and we probably need to be there to make sure. Is that okay?"

Dorothy tried to hide her excitement. "Whatever you think is best, Lionel."

Once again, Bob Pierce spoke about God's grace and the gift of eternal life in the person of Jesus Christ, explaining that all you need to do is receive it as a free gift from God. With every word, he seemed to be speaking directly to them. *You,* Dorothy Mayell, and *you,* Lionel Mayell, God loves you so much and has a wonderful plan for your life. It's not about what you can *do* for Him, it's about a relationship *with* Him.

The service was coming to an end. Dorothy wanted so much to know this God. So did Lionel. Still, she vowed not to make a move. What if Lionel knew she wasn't a Christian?

Then he took her hand as tears ran down his face. "I don't know this Jesus. Do you?"

She shook her head. "No, honey, but I want this more than anything in my entire life."

The search they did not even know they were on, was over.

On the second Saturday night in 1944 at the Youth for Christ meeting held at the Church of the Open Door, Dorothy and Lionel walked hand in hand to the front. Bob Pierce, the fiery evangelist who had again delivered the message, prayed with them to receive Christ. From then on, everything was different.

They continued to attend the Youth for Christ meetings, and grew in their relationship with Christ and with one another. They would pray and read the Bible together, and learned how to hear God speak to their hearts. In May of 1945, they celebrated the birth of their first child together, a daughter named after Dorothy.

Shortly afterward, Lionel shared with his wife that he desired to get back into building his own-your-own apartments on a deed basis. They both knew that God had called them together as partners for some greater destiny. As well, rumors had been circulating around Douglas Aircraft about a new piece of hardware that could end the war, possibly before year's end. If those rumors were true, now might be the time to take that first step.

Together, they knelt and prayed, "Lord Jesus, we don't have any money, and we can't start a business over again without money. This business is going to be for your honor and glory." The next morning over breakfast, they prayed again and asked God for His mercy, protection, and guidance as Lionel stepped out in faith to talk to his bank. He dressed in his Sunday best and went to the Bank of America office on the corner of Highland Avenue and Hollywood Boulevard to talk to the bank manager.

He began, "Mr. Hammond, you don't know me, but I used to build apartments in Long Beach and Los Angeles and other places in the twenties. I was forced to stop building because of the Great Depression and war, but I want to start building again.

For the past four years, I have worked at Douglas Aircraft and have continued to conduct all my banking business with you. Working at Douglas, I've been privy to information about a new piece of war hardware that will bring Japan to its knees. I want to build again, and want to see how much money I can borrow from you in an unsecured note to start over again."

Without hesitating, Mr. Hammond responded, "Lionel Mayell, I know you and your accomplishments in construction, and I would gladly let you borrow anytime on an unsecured note even without your wife's signature."

Lionel could not speak. He had prepared his case and had expected to spend a great deal of effort convincing the bank to loan him money. Although Germany had surrendered in May, the country was still at war with Japan and the outcome was not yet assured.

Mr. Hammond continued, "I also know your character, and would like to extend to you a loan for one thousand dollars to start over."

Lionel couldn't wait to share the miraculous news with Dorothy. He raced home on Cloud Nine. "Dorothy darling, Rosebud, where are you?" Lionel's voice echoed in the large foyer of their home. "I have exciting news! Quick!"

Dorothy ran down the stairs. "Oh, Lionel, I've been praying. What happened? Is everything all right?"

They sat down in the kitchen, and he recounted his time at the bank. "Dorothy, I know for sure that the war must be over soon and I can start to build again. This time I will build differently. I threw my money away in show business. I was foolish and left God out. Not anymore. I know that God let Mr. Hammond believe in me. It had to be God. Who gets to borrow on an unsecured note and is told that anytime he can secure a loan? One thousand dollars isn't much, but it's still unheard of. The Depression has subsided, and I was told on the spot I could borrow money. I want to make good money and get out of this poverty so I can properly take care of you and the children."

She also had something to share: "I've been praying the entire time you've been gone, and I, too, know that this is from God. He told me that He was going to bless your business. Now, Daddy, I'm going to say this: When you get the one thousand dollars, I want you to divide that between two accounts. Five hundred dollars will go into our general account for business to start the new project, and the other five hundred is to be put into the Lord's Account to honor Him with our giving and do a great work. That is what I want to suggest."

"But, Mother, what can I do with a measly five hundred dollars?"

"You can do more with five hundred dollars with God's blessing than with one thousand dollars without," she replied. "I believe that this gesture will prove that we have made the Lord Jesus Christ our business partner."

"But I'm already struggling to see how I can even begin to build a business with one thousand dollars. I have no other choice. Tomorrow, I'm going to put all the money into the idle Mayell Enterprises business account. Dorothy, the Lord made this arrangement in answer to our prayers and certainly does not expect any part of it in return. It's all going into the Mayell business account in the morning."

Dorothy sighed. "Lionel, you do what God tells you to do, but again let me say that I would rather be in business with God with five hundred dollars than be in business without Him with a thousand." She felt strongly that her suggestion was right but was willing to be wrong. For the first time in her life, she had stepped out and trusted God to work.

The next morning, Lionel was up early and dressed in his best Sunday suit, quietly singing while he prepared a queen's breakfast for Dorothy: scrambled eggs and sliced grapefruit fresh from the backyard citrus trees.

"Lionel, you let me sleep in," she said when he carried her breakfast into the bedroom. "What's going on? You're so dressed up."

"You were right and I was wrong," he admitted. "We did promise to have God as our partner, and even though I could try to justify opening one account and inviting God to bless it, that's not what I believe God is asking of me. I couldn't do this without you being by my side. Thank you, darling, for always bringing me back to what is right. I would like us to pray together as we take this step. I don't know how God is going to do this, but I know this is the right thing."

As recorded in notes, Lionel prayed, "Dear Lord, from the bottom of my heart, I not only want to thank you for making my conversation possible with the bank manager, but for his gracious accepting spirit. In the first place, you made him happy and willing to give me the loan I needed. In the second place, you had him treat me in a wonderful way, demonstrating once again your love for me and my family. Thank you again for helping me in this piece of business and for the great mightiness you are doing and are going to continue to do in our lives for your honor and glory as well as for our own happiness."

On that day in 1945, two separate accounts were opened at the Bank of America with Dorothy as cosigner and partner. One for Mayell Enterprises and the other titled "Lord's Account." The beginning balance in each account was $500.

While at the Youth for Christ meeting a few nights later, Lionel felt led to make the first contribution out of the Lord's Account into the Lord's work. Bob Pierce and Dave Morken were the speakers for the evening. Lionel was a new believer, but he sensed an urgent prompting from the Holy Spirit. Removing the checkbook from his pocket, he wrote out a check payable to Youth for Christ for $500, the entire amount in the account. In the left-hand corner he wrote, "To start Youth for Christ in the Orient." He then discreetly handed the check to Dorothy so she could co-sign it.

"Why give all the money we have in that account to start work in the Orient when no one's said anything about starting Youth for Christ in the Orient?" she whispered.

Lionel smiled. "Please sign it."

"But this seems to be foolish, darling. Why do that? Let's just give twenty-five dollars or a different amount, but not all the money at once."

"Dorothy, please just sign it."

Reluctantly, she signed the check, and he placed it in the offering plate.

One week later, Bob Pierce and David Morken were speaking three thousand miles away at a Youth for Christ meeting in St. Petersburg, Florida. It was an outdoor rally, held in a park with thousands in attendance braving a soaking Florida rainstorm to hear the gospel. They told a story about a young couple back in Los Angeles who had just sacrificed to give them a check for $500 to start Youth for Christ in the Orient, a dream they had been praying about for five years but had never spoken of before. Youth for Christ had received many invitations over the years to start a ministry in China, but they had no money to do so. This $500 check, which Lionel was supernaturally led to write, was an answer to years of prayer.

At the end of the evening, an elderly man approached David Morken with a rain-soaked envelope in his hand. "Read this after the meeting," he said as he handed him the envelope.

David Morken tucked it away in his topcoat.

During the middle of the night, he awakened and remembered the envelope. Retrieving his topcoat from the closet, he pulled out the envelope and opened it to find a check inside. The ink had begun to run on the check, but he could see that it was a cashier's check in the amount of $5,000. Written on the left-hand side of the check was the notation "To help start the work of Youth for Christ in the Orient." The date on the check was the same day as the meeting in St. Petersburg; the man's daughter had secured the check from the bank prior to the meeting.

Two separate individuals, three thousand miles apart, had each been led to give sacrificially for a cause they had never heard about. The man's check for $5,000 and Lionel and Dorothy's check for $500 became the seed money that started Youth for Christ in China and Korea before the Chinese Communist Revolution closed off the territory. Thousands of orphans were saved after World War II, and Youth for Christ in the Orient later became the ministry we now know as World Vision.

Dorothy and Lionel's Lord's Account would be replenished many times over, and the remaining $500 in the Mayell Enterprises business account was about to launch a condominium empire worth hundreds of millions of dollars.

On August 6, 1945, the United States dropped a uranium gun-type atomic bomb (Little Boy) on Hiroshima, Japan. Three days later, a plutonium implosion-type bomb (Fat Man) was dropped on Nagasaki. These atomic bombs were the rumored "war hardware" that Lionel had heard about at Douglas Aircraft. On September 2, 1945, World War II came to an end.

———

This story speaks of boldness.

The boldness of a housekeeper to challenge my dad's faith. Randy was a quiet woman whose family had kicked her out for being a believer. Out of compassion, my dad gave her free room and board, and out of gratitude, Randy requested that she clean Mom and Dad's house. She had the courage to ask a question that initially returned an indignant response but ultimately resulted in my dad and mom attending the youth meeting that forever changed their hearts and their lives.

And the boldness of faith of my mother to adamantly propose a fifty-fifty partnership with the Lord, and the boldness of my father to ask for a loan in a recovering economy following the Depression and the war. For the first time in their lives, Mom and Dad encountered the real gospel of Jesus Christ, one full of grace and mercy that cut through all the religion of their past and ignited an undeniable love and power.

· C H A P T E R   T E N ·

GOD DID IT

FOR THE CHURCH, THE 1940s were the most dramatic and significant years of the twentieth century. This transformational period birthed an evangelical resurgence across the nation. God was doing something profound, and for the first time, the gospel was not just for adults but also for the youth.

Also during this time, the word *teenager* was coined, but with the war going on, no one paid much attention. Adolescents were expected to act like adults, and many boys hardly old enough to shave had been shipped off to war. Sociologists saw the youth culture as something to research, and the public took notice. The youth wanted their own styles, and they weren't interested in church.

Even before the war, God was causing pastors all over the world to see the need to reach the youth with the gospel. A former dance-band trombonist named Jack Wyrtzen launched a radio broadcast in Manhattan called "Word of Life Hour." Although he never graduated from high school, he became a pioneer in

Christian radio and gave birth to a new wave of evangelical preaching to youth—a blend of dynamic music, powerful testimonies, and short preaching. Teaming up with well-known evangelist Jack Shuler, musician George Beverly Shea, and others, Jack Wyrtzen and his Saturday-night rallies routinely packed out venues such as Carnegie Hall and Madison Square Garden with over twenty thousand in attendance and ten thousand turned away. People were in desperate need of hope.

His innovative methods of youth evangelism served as a pattern for many other evangelical parachurch organizations, and, in particular, proved to be a moving force in the early stages of Youth for Christ. The term *youth* included everyone who wasn't married and married people who considered themselves young. The meetings helped kindle a fire for youth evangelism nationwide, and rising youth evangelists began their own Youth for Christ rallies in all the major cities. By the fall of 1942, Torrey Johnson, pastor of Midwest Bible Church, was invited to start Youth for Christ in Chicago. Bob Pierce, an evangelist in Southern California, became involved with the Los Angeles Youth for Christ movement and was a regular speaker at the rallies held at the Church of the Open Door.

By 1944, nothing was bigger or more influential than Youth for Christ. Every well-known preacher in America preached at Youth for Christ rallies in Chicago that summer, including Billy Graham, R. G. LeTourneau, Harry Ironside, Wendell Loveless, and V. R. Edmond. The rallies filled Orchestra Hall every Saturday night, and they routinely had to turn people away.

Inquiries flooded into Chicago about starting Youth for Christ rallies in eighteen cities across America. The fire was spreading, and it was obvious that this movement was of God.

In the middle of it all was Torrey Johnson, a bold, unconventional sparkplug who held it all together. That fall, Youth for Christ held a victory rally in Chicago Stadium with over twenty-thousand attendees.

The next year, 1945, was a year to remember. Germany surrendered to the Allied forces in May. Japan surrendered several months later. Americans danced in the streets. The Depression was over, the war had pulled the country together, and optimism grew. Young men and women began returning home, full of energy and a spirit of "let's get things done."

In an all-night prayer meeting, Torrey Johnson proclaimed, "O God, we want this kept on a miracle basis. We want everyone to know that God's hand is on this movement. We want folks to see that this is too big and too great for any man or group of men to accomplish by themselves. We want folks to say, 'God did it!'"

And God's hand was clearly on the movement. Torrey Johnson mortgaged his house to get the money to rent Soldier Field, and on Memorial Day, just three weeks after V-E Day (Victory in Europe), Youth for Christ held the "mother of all youth rallies," with a five-thousand-voice choir, a three-hundred-piece band, and more than seventy thousand in attendance.

The movement attracted media attention, and two months later, Youth for Christ made it official by electing Torrey Johnson its first president. With his fiery personality, he became the flag-bearer for the movement. His first full-time hire was Billy Graham, who was on demand to speak at rallies all over the country. Soon afterward, he hired Cliff Barrows.

On October 7, 1945, eighteen thousand people packed out the Hollywood Bowl for a rally with Jack Shuler preaching.

One thousand decisions for Christ were made. Youth evangelism led revival in America, and it exponentially grew by leaps and bounds.

A year later in 1946, Torrey Johnson organized a second Memorial Day Soldier Field rally with seventy-five thousand in attendance and Charles Fuller as the speaker. When it started pouring rain, Charles Fuller stood up and calmly said, "Please close your umbrellas. We're going to ask God to stop the rain." He prayed, and the rain stopped.

That same year, David Morken began Youth for Christ in and around Shanghai, China. In the dramatic days of the following year, at least thirty thousand were won to Christ in the communist nation. He was joined in China by Bob Pierce as the Youth for Christ movement spread throughout Europe. Bob Pierce would eventually start two major international ministries, World Vision and Samaritan's Purse.

To support the tremendous wave of young people now wanting a biblical education, evangelicals founded sixty new Bible colleges between 1940 and 1950. Scores of significant parachurch ministries were begun as the Holy Spirit initiated creative vision on how to reach a lost and hurting world for Christ. Included were Christian Business Men's Committee (CBMC); Young Life; The Navigators; Fuller Theological Seminary; "The Word of Life Hour"; the Far East Broadcasting Company; Gospel Films, Inc.; Mission Aviation Fellowship; The Moody Institute; and a host of others.

The moment they accepted Jesus at a Youth for Christ rally in 1944, Lionel and Dorothy Mayell were placed on the ground floor of what God was doing in America. They were hungry to know this Jesus, and they grew in their relationship with Christ and their desire to place Him at the center of their lives. They continued attending Youth for Christ meetings and the Church of the Open Door. Their friendships with David and Helen Morken and Bob and Lorraine Pierce and their families deepened as they shared fellowship on a weekly basis over meals in each other's homes. Torrey Johnson encouraged them in their faith and exhorted them to dream the dreams that appeared to be too big for anyone but God.

As Lionel and Dorothy's relationship with Christ grew, so did their desire to give financially. They believed in giving back to the Lord and they tithed faithfully, but their desire to be even more generous intensified. They prayed and sought what they could do. Their budget was tight, as they had three children and the financial responsibility of two homes (Una had left them the homes but tied up the money in the children's names). They tried to sell one home with no success because the market was poor.

Lionel and Dorothy recognized that God was the One who had placed the desire in their hearts to give more generously. They explored ideas for starting other businesses that would enable them to give the profit solely to ministry. One of those businesses was a chicken farm. But the chicken farm quickly required far more financial investment and time than the little profit it generated, so they quickly sold out.

At every turn, they seemed to hit a wall. As a last resort, they decided to stop trying and give it to the Lord. They told Him they trusted Him and that He would have to figure it out, then agreed not to talk about it until they heard from God and both agreed about what He was saying.

Soon afterward, an idea came to Dorothy while she was running errands. In her excitement, she could hardly get home fast enough to talk with Lionel in his back-room office. "I know what we can do for the Lord," she told him. "Out-of-town guest speakers are staying in hotels for the weekends. God has given us this beautiful large home, and we have lots of extra rooms we don't use. Let us take one of our suites with private bath and call it our 'Prophet's Chamber' for the different evangelists and speakers."

Lionel loved the idea. "Let's do it right now."

And so, the private guest quarters at the Spanish Mediterranean estate at 684 South June Street in Los Angeles was set aside as the Prophet's Chamber. As they continued to pray together, they took yet another step by dedicating their entire home to the Lord. In this simple desire to give of their resources, God was orchestrating a blessing that would prepare them for the next stage of their lives, and for decades to come. Lionel and Dorothy took steps toward rebuilding Mayell Enterprises, and God began unfolding a plan that was abundantly more than they could dream or ask.

The Prophet's Chamber became the home away from home for every major evangelist and Bible teacher who traveled to Los Angeles over the next decade. These people were giants of the faith who God had called to be on the cutting edge of the explosive evangelical movement of the 1940s and 1950s, including Billy Graham and his entire crusade team; Torrey Johnson; R. G. LeTourneau; and Lewis Sperry Chafer, founder of Dallas Theological Seminary. Other notable guests included Richard Halverson, who later became the chaplain for the U.S. Senate; Dawson Trotman, founder of The Navigators; Wilbur Smith; Raymond Edman; Oswald Smith; Bob Bowman, founder of Far East Broadcasting; Ted Engstrom; and other noted evangelists and teachers of the day.

Almost every week for the next several years, from Thursday night through Sunday, a different evangelist or teacher was a guest in the Mayell home. But they were more than just house guests; they were also mentors to Lionel and Dorothy who, as new believers, had an insatiable hunger to know Jesus. They sat for hours with these powerful men and women of faith, asking questions and absorbing truth, while the seeds of His life were being rooted and grounded in their hearts. Most importantly, these times of fellowship and mentoring ignited the gift of faith in Dorothy and Lionel, a faith they would need for the battle just around the corner.

Before the war, Pasadena, like Long Beach, had been primarily a winter resort for wealthy Easterners. Great tourist hotels and magnificent seasonal mansions were built, centering on South Orange Grove Boulevard, which gained a national reputation as Pasadena's version of Millionaire's Row. The one-and-a-quarter-mile stretch from Colorado Boulevard to Columbia Street was said to be one of the most beautiful residential streets in America, and was the starting point for the famed Tournament of Roses Parade. Every home was a mansion set far back from the street and surrounded by beautifully landscaped gardens and vast lawns.

After World War II, Pasadena became more of a year-round city. As new sections developed and the population grew, a lot of the older areas became run down. Well-to-do visitors stayed away, leaving many of the most elaborate winter estates unoccupied. Although few families cared to maintain the old mansions, South Orange Grove Boulevard retained substantial social cachet. What it seemed to require was a new kind of housing—in particular, well-equipped, owner-occupied multi-family housing.

Lionel Mayell was the first to recognize the changing social and economic landscape. After the war, he had begun acquiring land in Pasadena as soon as labor and materials were released for real estate development. He launched his first two cooperative apartment projects in 1947 and 1948, and in the spring of 1948, he took out a permit to replace a mansion on South Orange Grove Boulevard with a modern, ultra-luxury own-your-own apartment court.

He understood something about Southern California that other developers, most of whom weren't West Coast natives, did not: Californians wanted a relaxed "Western" lifestyle with lots of light, relationship to the outdoors, and easy access to the automobile. The East Coast's congested high-rise model wasn't appealing to well-to-do Californians. Lionel, even in his earlier resort-style own-your-owns in Long Beach in the 1920s had realized this, and employed an open-concept architectural design that allowed plenty of light, air, and sweeping panoramic views from each apartment.

Over the years, many trends have begun in Southern California and worked their way across the country. The trend in housing preferences in the 1940s and 1950s was no different. People had been moving to California in droves over the previous decades, mostly because of its mild, sunny climate and reputation for being the land of opportunity, but also because it became a hub of aviation, aerospace, and auto-making activity during wartime.

Southern California was quickly becoming densely populated, and the suburban single-family "dream" home had become a reality for many Californians long before the rest of the country. People were now ready for something different.

Demographics were changing, households were getting smaller and non-traditional, and the cost of living in a large, elaborate home was escalating. Living in a smaller home became appealing even to well-to-do people, but they wanted to own and not rent. Medium density owner-occupied multi-family housing became popular, and Lionel was the first to recognize the changing paradigm.

He wasn't the only developer wanting to build; the difference was in *how* he wanted to build. His apartment court would require a zoning change, from single-family to restricted residential (R-R). His idea was new and fresh, and he thought it would be easy to gain approval to build. But Lionel was about to enter what newspapers would describe as a "civil war." He had never witnessed such viciousness in business, and he would need the assurance of a loving God that he was right in the middle of His will.

Even as far back as the Depression years, there was a growing sense that the heyday of old South Orange Grove Boulevard was over. The fight had been raging for years, and the zoning study was said to be the longest and most expensive one in U.S. history. In 1942, the *Los Angeles Herald Express* reported that there was a "civil war in Pasadena over the proposed rezoning of South Orange Grove Avenue. Residents of South Orange Grove Avenue clashed bitterly and oratorically in arguments for and against the proposed rezoning of this famous avenue for swanky height-limit apartment houses. Many of them were making the last stand for the aristocratic old time Pasadena."[9]

At times, the controversy became heated. The *Herald Express* observed the sentiments of the homeowners: "This is a city of homes and we don't want to be jammed in. We left our homes of

Chicago and other cities because there were too many people. Do not kid yourselves that putting up multiple housing apartments is going to beautify Orange Grove Avenue or take us back to the good ol' days."[10]

Leet Bissell, owner of the Bissell family mansion and speaking for the South Orange Grove Avenue Association in February of 1948, said that "any poll would reveal that the majority of property owners living on the street opposed any change in zoning which would permit what he terms 'three-story monstrosities for the benefit of greedy developers.'"[11]

On April 6, 1948, the *Pasadena Star-News* noted that the sentiment among property owners was still divided about fifty-fifty over the proposed R-R zone. Voters in favor of the rezoning pointed out that most of the people who lived in the mansions could no longer sustain their homes and were going to board out rooms. The mansions were only going to be preserved by converting them into boarding houses with no guidelines to promise their upkeep. Some predicted that South Orange Grove Avenue would become a row of boarding houses unless the new zoning plan was adopted.[12]

The opposition was fierce, and Lionel Mayell appeared before the City Planning Commission and the homeowners time after time. The controversy was finally settled a month later in May 1948 when the City Planning Commission approved a restricted residential zone for South Orange Grove Avenue, and granted Mayell Enterprises special permission to construct the first apartments on Millionaires' Row.[13]

The following year, construction began on Orange Grove Manor, as reported March 27, 1949 in the *Pasadena Star-News:* "Pasadena's famed South Orange Grove Avenue, the West's most famous residential thoroughfare, gets the 'new look' next month when construction starts on Lionel V. Mayell's cooperative restricted residences to be known as 'Orange Grove Manor.'"[14]

In a sign posted on the building site, a promise was made to the city: "In answer to many requests from people who have expressed a desire to live on South Orange Grove Avenue, we offer Orange Grove Manor and we promise that our buildings and landscaping will be a real asset to Pasadena's most beautiful residential street. —Lionel V. Mayell, March 27, 1949."[15]

Initially, the newspapers weren't very supportive of the change. The *Los Angeles Times* reported that "in the midst of disdainful mansions and the frowning ghosts of a thousand blue-blooded memories, the first units of an apartment colony are being erected. A big sign beckons to those who would invade 'Millionaire's Row,' which is reserved for millionaires no more."[16] Another newspaper announced that "Lionel Mayell, an intense little fellow (five feet, one inches tall), a rapid-fire conversationalist who pours himself into his words as though in an attempt to make up for his lack of size, has successfully jumped in front of well-known builders with his unique garden plan of cooperatives, breaking the century-old zoning ordinance against multiple dwelling in Pasadena's exclusive neighborhood of Millionaire's Row."

Lionel made good on his promise to the city. His cutting-edge garden-type apartment homes proved to have exactly what prospective home buyers were looking for—sweeping vistas and indoor-outdoor living with landscaped gardens, privacy, and exclusiveness. Orange Grove Manor consisted of a cluster of five two-story multiple-unit buildings in the Minimal Traditional style, a blend of traditional and period-contemporary architectural styling with influences of Colonial Revival architecture that was so well executed that the street view could have easily passed for one of the previous mansions on Millionaire's Row.

With a front setback of more than forty feet, the buildings were clad in smooth stucco with brick accents and had a composition-shingle hip roof, bow windows in front, multi-pane steel casement windows, rectangular plan bays, paneled doors, and brick chimneys. Each unit included private garage parking. Orange Grove Manor represented a great advance in the evolution of middle-class housing in Southern California.

Lionel's astute recognition of the post-war climate, and his innovative pairing of garden style courtyard apartment living with the social and financial benefits of home ownership, transformed the owner-occupied apartment from a marginal experiment into a desirable year-round home. It took a few years, but by 1954 the *Los Angeles Times* had reversed its negative position. A society columnist reported, "Many people who have lived in their own homes for years are moving into 'own-your-own' apartments."[17]

Today, Orange Grove Manor is designated a Pasadena Historic Landmark, and in 2015, the property sold for hundreds of thousands of dollars over the listing price of $9.5 million. Besides the historical significance, Orange Grove Manor is highly attractive because of its character and unique features. The most-valued amenities are the wood-burning fireplaces, hardwood floors, crown moulding, front and rear entrances, and average size of 1,300 square feet.

South Orange Grove Avenue remains a beautiful residential street, with only a few of the mansions left that once gave it fame throughout the nation. The "civil war" that preceded the transition and the former grandeur of Millionaires' Row are now part of the colorful history of early Pasadena.

In Jeremiah 29:11, God declares that the purpose and plans He has are to prosper us and not harm us, to give us hope and a good future. God created each of us with a purpose and plan, and infused in us a piece of Himself along with a dream of how to best display that part of Himself to the world. It is up to Him to lead us in discovering His dream, to equip us to be fully prepared for our purpose and destiny.

Mom and Daddy were perfectly imperfect people, but they learned to depend upon God's love, strength, and voice for the next step. God did the rest. He designed and placed specific desires and timing in their hearts. He connected them to the right people and situations that would fully prepare them for success, and even used their failures and mistakes as part of their development.

God did it all. And He longs to do the same for each of us today.

Orange Grove Manor, Pasadena, CA

CHAPTER ELEVEN

THE BUILDER OF DREAMS

W ITH THE ZONING VICTORY that led to Orange Grove Manor, Lionel Mayell had won the toughest battle of his career. His mother was gone, and there was no one to fall back on for financial support.

No one, that is, except God. This journey for Lionel was a new experience, one of faith and a personal relationship with a loving God whom he and Dorothy had declared would be their partner in rebuilding his business. For the first time, Lionel really understood the meaning of the verse he borrowed from John Wanamaker in the 1920s: "For God is a rewarder of those that diligently seek Him." The difference was, he began to diligently seek *Him*, rather than diligently seek the *reward*.

And God did reward, according to His plan. The zoning battle over South Orange Grove Boulevard had been going on since the Depression and before the war, and long before Lionel was saved and even before he began his first construction career in the 1920s. That building site, and that zoning battle, had been reserved for him. And the vision that became Orange Grove Manor had been formed in Lionel's mind by none other than a loving God.

After he was awarded the rezoning permit and began construction in 1948, Lionel became sought after for projects, speaking engagements, and board positions. One such opportunity was introduced through his friend R. G. LeTourneau, a prominent Christian businessman and inventor from Dallas and a frequent speaker with Youth for Christ.

R. G. LeTourneau was a frequent guest in the Mayells' home, occupying the Prophet's Chamber when in the Los Angeles area to speak for various events. He was perhaps the most prolific inventor of earth-moving equipment in the 1920s and 1930s, someone who changed the world both then and now with his contributions to road construction and heavy machinery. Famous for living on 10 percent of his income and giving 90 percent to advance the spread of the gospel, he served as an inspiring business role model for Lionel.

R. G. LeTourneau introduced Lionel to the CBMC, an organization that started in Chicago in 1930 to encourage businessmen in their Christian walk and empower them to share their faith in the marketplace. He was so impressed with Lionel's journey of faith that he gave Lionel's name to several key leaders across Southern California as a possible speaker. Soon Lionel was traveling to various CBMC breakfasts and giving his testimony of how he had been in show business, lost everything, and then found Jesus.

At one such occasion, Lionel had been invited by Lawrence Young, chairman of CBMC Hollywood, to speak at their breakfast at the Pig and Whistle Coffeehouse on Hollywood Boulevard.

The members were captivated by his story, but time ran short and all voted to have him return the following week to finish his testimony. The next week's meeting coincided with the annual election of officers for CBMC Hollywood. The floor was open for recommendations for who should be the next chairman, and Lionel, who had just finished speaking, was nominated by three members.

There was just one problem: the CBMC guidelines required that officers be a member, which Lionel was not. The three members who nominated him were not aware of the stipulation, but the current officers decided not to withdraw his name from consideration. At the close of the meeting, the results of the election were tabulated and Lionel had been unanimously voted in as the new chairman.

He stood and, with tears streaming down his face, stammered, "I can't be the chairman. I'm not even a member."

Lawrence Young rose to his feet and faced him. With conviction and assurance, he said, "Lionel Mayell, you've been duly elected by the membership as the chairman of the Hollywood CBMC for this next year. God has placed you in this role, and I personally count it as a privilege to work beside you as together we will draw many non-Christians to Christ, and encourage every businessman to grow in their faith."

CBMC Hollywood tripled in size that next year, and for the next six years Lionel was re-elected to the position of chairman. He was also asked to be on the board of Christ for Greater Los Angeles, during which time he was influential in bringing Billy Graham to the Youth for Christ rally in the Hollywood Bowl in 1947 and the famous long-running Crusade of Greater Los Angeles the following year. Lionel and Dorothy were witnessing miracles all around them in the late 1940s, and the miraculous was becoming the norm for everyday life.

Mayell Enterprises experienced a major breakthrough with Orange Grove Manor. Lionel and Dorothy had a second chance to rebuild their business, and they took the idea of being in partnership with God and applied it to every area of their business. They dedicated a supply closet in the sales office of Orange Grove Manor as their "Prayer Room." In the closet were two folding chairs, a Bible, large sheets of paper, and colorful markers. Their "Prayer Wall" was plastered with pieces of paper bearing written goals and needs of Mayell Enterprises, and the name of every potential buyer plus their family members.

Lionel and Dorothy prayed over each goal and gave it to the Lord. When someone came to look at an apartment, they prayed over that potential buyer, sometimes praying together and sometimes taking turns. Every construction worker employed on the project and every delivery person was prayed over by name. They dedicated every part of the project in prayer, and invited God to take charge.

By the time Orange Grove Manor was finished, it was completely sold out. That was highly unusual for such a speculative development. Lionel had taken a risk on the project, but with God as his business partner, the risk was in His hands. As people saw the quality of workmanship, modern features, unparalleled location, attractive views, and custom-designed interiors, they became interested in the idea of a Lionel Mayell own-your-own. Orange Grove Manor proved to be so beautiful that the same people who fought his development—the Pasadena Planning Commission and the millionaire homeowners' community—begged Lionel to develop more properties on their famous street, this time with their unanimous blessing.

And he did. Again, and again, and again.

Over the next ten years, Lionel completed as many as ten additional complexes in Pasadena, including four more on Millionaire's Row—155 and 255 South Orange Grove Boulevard, 707 South Orange Grove Boulevard, and Capri Aire.

To be closer to the new building projects, Lionel and Dorothy sold their home on South June Street in Los Angeles and moved to the neighboring community of Altadena. He was a visionary and had big dreams, but he believed God's dreams were even bigger. Both he and Dorothy agreed they would put 30 percent of their total gross income into the Lord's Account, and it replenished quickly. Giving more was not anything anyone told them to do, but after they prayed, they wanted to give generously from a joyful heart. And the more they gave, the more opportunities came their way to earn.

For each new project, the first room to be established in the office was the Prayer Room. And it was in the Prayer Room that God granted Lionel the vision for new and innovative "firsts" that became his trademark. Each new development was better equipped with richer materials and newer technologies than the last. For example, in 1953, Villa San Pasqual consisted of fifteen modernistic buildings grouped around two courts. Each of the sixty suites had a kitchen finished in natural birch with copper hardware and sixteen-foot-wide sliding glass balcony or patio doors on silent nylon roller bearings.

This was also Lionel's first air-conditioned project, and each home was selected by its future owner prior to completion. He brought in green slate roof shingles from Idaho to complement the buildings' stucco facades, which he painted flamingo pink. Over fifty years later, in 2005, Villa San Pasqual was honored with Historic Landmark status by the city of Pasadena for its fine example of mid-century architecture.

In 1954, Lionel financed and built the Plaza del Arroyo and introduced a dramatic water feature, Pasadena's only multicolored fountain. Five four-unit buildings were arranged around lush lawns, with commanding views overlooking the Rose Bowl, the Arroyo Seco River, and the Colorado Street Bridge. The fountain caused the city of Pasadena to extend to Lionel a meritorious citation for his contribution to the beautification of the city.

Plaza del Arroyo featured detached two-car garages and storage, front and rear balconies, period tile bathrooms, hardwoods, open floor plans, king-sized bedrooms, spacious walk-in closets, and fireplaces. It was so popular that over 90 percent of the units sold before the first building was 50 percent completed.

While Lionel didn't invent the post-war garden-type apartment, he very well may have perfected it, and he most certainly popularized it. He became known for his choice locations, and made it accessible and desirable, even fashionable, for the middle and upper-middle classes to forego a single-family home in favor of an own-your-own apartment. A *Los Angeles Times* article published in 1954 listed the names of well-known judges, doctors, lawyers, authors, and celebrities who had chosen to buy a Mayell Enterprises home.

Beyond quality workmanship, Lionel established his company policies to reflect his Christian faith, policies not usually found in other businesses or industries. No work was done on Sunday, both in building construction and sales. He had a firm rule of no-pressure sales. His senior leadership team and business partners were all hand-selected executives that God had connected through ministry with Youth for Christ and CBMC. His letterhead, all his collateral material, and his office door reflected the following dedication: "Except the Lord build the house, they labor in vain that build it. —Psalm 127:1. The management and personnel of Lionel V. Mayell Enterprises acknowledge with grateful thanks the continued blessing of Almighty God upon our endeavors. We reaffirm our dependence on Him for daily blessing and guidance ... and to reflect His love in our dealings for those who produce our homes and those who purchase them."

As Lionel's reputation spread, he received invitations from other cities to bring his popular own-your-own concept to their community. In 1955, he began organizing corporations in other cities in Southern California, and within the next eight years amassed a building empire worth almost $100 million and spanning four states. The dreamer became known as the "Builder of Dreams." The term *Mayell-built* gained cachet as he became one of America's best-known residential developers. Professionally, his rise was meteoric, as he moved prominently among representatives of the building trades where he was reputed for his wide knowledge about what people wanted in home buying.

Each new project became bigger, more elaborate, and more expensive than the last. Lionel rarely employed architects, relying instead on engineers to plan his buildings, and following his own design concepts. In the late 1950s, he had as many as nine projects going on at one time, in eight cities across three states.

Increasingly, garden-type multi-family homes proved to be what home buyers were looking for, so Lionel sought to improve them. He added the lanai terrace, with floor-to-ceiling sliding glass exterior walls; he introduced water landscaping, utilizing large irregular-shaped pools of filtered, constantly recirculating water with multiple large fountains and fountain jets as the principle exterior feature; and he introduced novel and attractive outside plate-glass elevators, as well as bathrooms with "ceilings of light."

His own thoughtful details were added: additional "sound-conditioning" between walls and customization options with free consultations with interior designers. He made standard what had formerly been considered "luxury" features found only in single-family homes: the latest appliances, all-electric kitchens, large closets, built-in storage, fireplaces, and other luxuries.

Lionel had a gift for communicating his own-your-own concept in a way that clearly differentiated it from other types of projects, most notably the Eastern ninety-nine-year-lease co-op model. Every brochure and advertisement captured the essence of the appeal: "You don't rent it, you own it. You get a clear title. No stock. No blanket mortgage. No fine print. No legal entanglement."

He highlighted the luxury and convenience of apartment living combined with the comfort, security, and benefits of home ownership. Pooled buying power of all the owners yielded substantial savings on insurance, utilities, maintenance, and landscape costs. He even promised a substantial profit on resales, which proved to be true, both at the time and still today. All things considered, Lionel helped transform the image of multi-family housing into a prestige choice.

Following the wildly successful Villa San Pasqual in Pasadena, Lionel built two nearly identical developments in Arizona, the Villa del Coronado in Phoenix (1955–1957) and the Villa Catalina in Tucson (1957–1961), plus a third Phoenix project, Palm Lane Gardens (1958). Each property was situated in the most beautiful section of the city and featured expansive use of plate-glass, semi-tropical landscaping around two large irregular-shaped pools punctuated by leaping multicolored fountains, and front and rear patios or balconies. To add a touch of comfort in the Arizona sun, each three-story building was equipped with its own air-conditioned elevator. The Villa Catalina in Tucson was listed in the National Register of Historic Places in 1999.

He built numerous other projects along the coast of Southern California. Near the exclusive community of La Jolla, he built Capri Aire (1958) and Villa del Lido (1958–1959). Because of the proximity to the ocean, he built a beach surrounding the extra-large tropical landscaped pool, with sand he imported directly from Hawaii.

At the same time, he developed north of Los Angeles in Santa Barbara and Palo Alto: Villa Capri Aire (1955), with views of both the ocean and mountains; Villa Constance (1958); and Villa Miradero (1963), which won honorable mention in "Today's Best in Apartment Design" sponsored by *House & Home* magazine in August of 1963.

Representing the superlative degree in Lionel Mayell's planning and design, Whispering Waters in Pasadena (1959–1961) was the first multi-family development to use water as a major landscape feature. It consisted of an extensive pond surrounding the entire front elevation of the property, setting the complex in a virtual moat of water. Acting as a transition from the busy urban street to the residences, the pond featured a series of six ring fountains at the center, and a fine spray of 1,600 jets of water lining the outer edge of the pool, all illuminated by a multicolored lighting scheme. The water feature also cooled the building's air conditioning system by recirculation. Here, Lionel introduced novel and attractive outdoor plate-glass elevators, the first ones known to be used in a residential setting.

During the same time, he also built Whispering Waters developments in three Florida cities: Winter Park, St. Petersburg, and Palm Beach Shores. Character-defining features included lush subtropical landscaping and island planters within the pond, cantilevered balcony floors that doubled as canopies, large sliding glass doors with gold-anodized aluminum frames, and decorative open metal railings. Whispering Waters in Pasadena, now a condominium complex, has been proposed for Historic Landmark status.

Lionel was also recognized for creative vision that extended beyond traditional multi-family housing. Long before seniors had suitable housing options, even seniors with money, he conceived an upscale "life-care residence" in Santa Barbara called The Samarkand (1955–1958), which means "heart's desire." He and his close friend, noted Christian psychologist Clyde Narramore, sold the idea of a high-class residence for Christian seniors to Southern California petroleum-magnate Otis Birch. Others in on the project included Charles Fuller and R. G. LeTourneau.

The Samarkand was made up of thirty-four elaborate villas surrounding a hotel-type central building and located on sixteen tropical landscaped acres in the Santa Barbara hills. The residence provided maintenance-free one- and two-bedroom luxury apartments, all meals, medical care, and chapel, recreation, and hobby facilities. Today, The Samarkand is operated by Covenant

Retirement Communities and remains one of California's premier retirement communities.

The last of Mayell Enterprise's developments, the crown jewel and his gift to Houston, Texas, was the Ambassador at Post Oak (1962). Conceived as a first-generation new-build condominium apartment-home development, the Ambassador was strategically located in the developing upscale suburb that later became Uptown Houston. The Ambassador at Post Oak was billed as "Condominium Living with a Touch of Sheer Elegance in the Old South Tradition." The distinctive architecture features eighteen gleaming-white three-story columns with a porte-cochere that spans an elegant circular drive.

The original concept for the Ambassador included four mid-rise buildings, a club house, and a thirty-six-story high-rise. Only one building was completed before Lionel left the building industry altogether, but as proof of his vision, the immediate area around the Ambassador now has over twenty-five mid- and high-rise condominium buildings. Unlike many of these, the Ambassador has substantial outdoor space and formal landscaped gardens, a hallmark of a Mayell-built property. The location is probably the best amenity of all; it is within walking distance of the prestigious Galleria Shopping Center and the sophisticated shops along Post Oak Boulevard.

Today, many of Lionel Mayell's buildings are more than sixty years old, and some are more than ninety years old. None have ever been torn down. Four of his buildings are listed in the National Register of Historic Places, and five have been honored with Historic Landmark status by the cities they helped define. All are recognized as superb examples of their architectural style and sought after for their features, quality workmanship, and attention to detail. Most are still prized for their prime locations, and many command a premium price.

In real estate listings for Mayell Enterprises homes, the copy often touts that the home was built by the "Father of the Condominium." And for many a purchaser over the decades, a Lionel Mayell apartment home was a dream that came true.

———

Mom and Dad continued to give money to launch the God-dreams that many carried in their hearts. And God rewarded Dad with a depth of wisdom, knowledge, and witty inventions (Proverbs 8:12) that catapulted his business beyond their wildest dreams. But God always does more than we expect or even dare to dream or imagine, and what He had in store for Mom and Dad would go beyond their money.

God was transitioning them into a ministry of greater influence, beyond the scope of building real estate to one of building and shaping hearts for eternal impact.

Whispering Waters, Pasadena

Mayell Enterprises Logo

VISION UNLEASHED

L IONEL AND DOROTHY HAD been faithful in little, and God had rewarded them much. From the beginning, they earmarked half of the $1,000 loan for the Lord's Account and used it to sow seeds, and God gave Lionel the creative vision and favor to be wildly successful in his business. The Lord's Account was replenished over and over.

From a simple idea like establishing a room in their home as the Prophet's Chamber, which grew out of their hearts' desire to give, Dorothy and Lionel were surrounded by the men and women God had called to lead the evangelical youth movement of the 1940s and 1950s, and were right where they could have the greatest impact for the kingdom. God intended to use Lionel for more than being a builder of dreams in residential construction; at the same time, He was equipping him with the vision and resources to be a builder of people, releasing God's dreams in others for the spread of the gospel around the world.

In an era when women were often stereotyped in demure, often subservient roles, Lionel was profoundly influenced in his Christian faith by strong women believers and teachers. The first was his mother, Una, who, despite her rigid focus on religion rather than a relationship, was a brilliant student of the Bible and an excellent speaker who exposed Lionel to Christian teachings, the study of Greek, and giants of the faith who would later be used by God in Lionel's own faith journey. Even though he didn't become a Christian until after Una died, Lionel was taking mental notes, and he could recall the details of her expository teachings of the Scriptures.

The second was his wife Dorothy, who was often the catalyst that encouraged Lionel to take a greater step of faith. After all, it was her idea to put half of the startup money for his construction business into the Lord's Account.

Another great woman God used in a powerful way was Henrietta Mears, one of the most influential Bible teachers of the twentieth century and Christian education director at First Presbyterian Church of Hollywood (Hollywood "Pres"). Lionel first met Henrietta when he attended Hollywood Pres during the time his mother would be invited to speak. Henrietta built one of the largest Sunday Schools in the world and wrote her own curriculum, which was in such high demand that she founded Gospel Light Publications in 1933.

Even though Lionel wasn't a Christian when they first met, he remained in contact with Henrietta Mears, and after he and Dorothy accepted Christ, they began attending Bible studies in her home. It was during one of these Bible studies that he reconnected with someone from a few years before—the same businessman who owned the candy factory across from his scooter-manufacturing facility, Bill Bright.

Bill Bright had been an agnostic when he came to California in 1944, but he began attending Hollywood Pres and came to know Christ through Henrietta Mears' teaching of the college group. Bill, now married to Vonette, had sold his candy business and was attending Fuller Seminary, not necessarily to pursue full-time Christian work but to learn more about God.

Henrietta Mears had become a mentor to Bill and Vonette, and she often said that she felt called to help them prepare for a great ministry that the Lord was working in their hearts. It wasn't immediately clear what that ministry would be, but over the next year, Dorothy and Lionel witnessed Bill and Vonette's hunger and growing passion for sharing Christ with young leaders.

Dorothy and Lionel often opened their home in Altadena as a place for UCLA students to have fun in the Olympic-sized pool, play football on the lawn, enjoy a home-cooked meal and homemade ice cream, and have an open forum to discuss their faith. Bill and Vonette volunteered to help, and enjoyed leading the discussions and sharing their faith with the students. They also volunteered to work with the youth at Hollywood Pres.

On the way home from Henrietta Mears' Bible study class one evening, Lionel looked at Dorothy, but before he could say a word, she said, "I know, Lionel. I thought the same thing."

"Darling, what did you think I was going to say?" he asked.

"You want to give money out of the Lord's Account to Bill and Vonette toward the vision and dream of full-time sharing Christ."

"Exactly. All we have done is pray, but somebody needs to step up and support God's dream. The problem is, we don't know exactly what the vision is, but we have definitely witnessed a calling on Bill and Vonette with students."

When they arrived home, they went into the den and prayed. This time Lionel suggested that each of them write down, on separate pieces of paper, what they thought they should give. When they revealed their number to each other, the amounts were identical. Lionel wrote a check emptying the Lord's Account again, and Dorothy co-signed.

The following week, they could hardly wait to attend the Bible study at Henrietta Mears' home. They arrived thirty minutes early, and were elated to find that the only ones there were Bill and Vonette. Taking Dorothy's hand in his, Lionel said, "Bill, I had no idea when we first met that neither of us knew the Lord. You became a Christian just a few months before I did. I was manufacturing toys and you were making candy, and now God has connected us again under new circumstances. Both Dorothy and I believe God would have us give this check to you as the start money for His dream and vision for your lives to share Christ full time."

Tears streamed down Bill's cheeks. "Lionel, you will never know what this means to us. I've been waiting for God's timing, and now I know—it is *now*. Vonette and I adore you and Dorothy, and we believe that one day the Lord will have us doing something very special together. We love you and Dorothy."

Lionel and Dorothy's check from the Lord's Account became the first seed money that in 1951 launched the world's largest Christian ministry, Campus Crusade for Christ. Years later, Vonette Bright shared with the author this conversation, and that Lionel and Dorothy's financial gift was the faith-builder and confirmation she needed to trust God and live by faith the rest of her life.

Bill Bright's words proved to be more prophetic than he could imagine; their lives and their ministries would forever be intertwined. Lionel emceed the first banquet of Campus Crusade for Christ along with Donn Moomaw, a UCLA center and linebacker who was later inducted in the Football Hall of Fame in 1973. Donn and Lionel teamed up so well that they were repeatedly asked to co-emcee banquets to promote the beginning of Campus Crusade for Christ. Donn later became the pastor of Los Angeles Bel Air Presbyterian Church, and gave both the invocation and benediction at Ronald Reagan's 1981 and 1985 presidential inaugurations.

With similar enthusiasm, Lionel put his energy, finances, and skill behind the vision of CBMC to accelerate its growth. CBMC committees grew at an explosive rate during the 1940s and began organizing citywide evangelistic crusades, the scale of which had not been seen since evangelist Billy Sunday was at his peak earlier in the century. CBMC was a new ministry on the West Coast, and Lionel felt it important for his chapter to catch the vision of what God was doing on the East Coast, where it first began.

After being elected president of CBMC Hollywood, Lionel's evangelical spirit was set ablaze. In addition to organizing and leading local banquets, he and Dorothy rented commercial buses and carried packed busloads of business acquaintances and their wives to various CBMC conventions and conferences as far away as Phoenix, the Grand Canyon, San Francisco, and Seattle, underwriting the entire trip. On these bus trips,

Lionel learned to share his faith and continued to be mentored by listening to the stories and testimonies of the men traveling to the conventions, as well as socializing with other chairmen from chapters all over the United States. One of those chapter presidents, Chuck Smith Sr., president of the Santa Anna CBMC, became a close friend and would lead singing on the bus trips.

Lionel prearranged, through the local police departments, to hold street meetings in various cities, and he secured nationally known speakers for the banquets, many of whom were friends from Youth for Christ: Jack Wyrtzen, Pulitzer prize-winning cartoonist Vaughn Shoemaker, and businessman Cliff Brannen from Sinclair Oil and R. G. LeTourneau's legal counsel. Over a period of eight years, these banquets resulted in thousands of first-time decisions for the Lord.

Because of his vision, tireless energy, and dedication, Lionel was elected CBMC chapter president in three cities—first in Hollywood and later in Los Angeles and Pasadena. While he was president of CBMC Pasadena, R. G. LeTourneau, who as president of CBMC International was in high demand to give his testimony, asked Lionel to take charge of planning which speaking engagements he should accept across Southern California. Rather than just hold another banquet, Lionel envisioned something on a much grander scale, an event that would reach many more people for Christ.

Lionel presented to the Pasadena leadership the idea of booking R. G. LeTourneau in the Pasadena Civic Auditorium, a nearly four-thousand-seat auditorium that was one of the most revered performance halls in the nation. Everyone was in favor of the idea, but there was just one obstacle, and it was a major one. The Pasadena CBMC, a young chapter, felt the cost to rent the large auditorium would be prohibitive. Lionel knew only one way to overcome obstacles, and that was to commit it to prayer.

Even before the front door shut behind him when he got home, Lionel called upstairs, his voice cracking with excitement, "Dorothy darling, I need you!"

"Lionel, is everything okay? What's wrong?"

"Nothing. I have a problem I need you to pray with me about to hear God's solution," he explained. "We would like to have R. G. Letourneau give his testimony at the Pasadena Civic Auditorium, but the members are fearful that the event is cost prohibitive. The auditorium is available for the night we need, and I know God wants CBMC there."

They knelt side by side, coming to the Lord in prayer. "Father, we trust you. You were the one who gave the vision and place and time for this banquet, and we believe you are the one who has the answer. We choose to believe like Joshua and Caleb, and see this as an opportunity for you to do what you already have placed in the leadership's hearts. Let us not walk in fear, but stand in faith with God-confidence."

Before Lionel could finish his prayer, Dorothy said softly, "Lionel, we have the money. God gave you the vision, so what about us just underwriting this night?"

He considered that. "Are you sure, honey?"

"I'm God-sure, Lionel. Now get up and let's do this. God is in charge of our checkbook. I would rather be in business with God than in any business endeavor without Him."

And so they did. Lionel worked with the local churches to publicize the event, and paid for several newspaper ads announcing R. G. LeTourneau as the keynote speaker. That evening in 1953, the Pasadena Civic Auditorium was filled to capacity. Merv

Rosell, a noted evangelist and the president of Youth for Christ, gave the altar call, and fifty-five people responded. Seated near the front of the auditorium, Lionel and Dorothy joined the new believers in rejoicing at the faithfulness of God.

Lionel and Dorothy understood the new converts' need to be connected to the larger body of Christ and to be mentored in their new profession of faith. It was vital to not just "get saved," but to strengthen one's faith and mature in Christ. This was not a church function and CBMC was not related to a particular denomination, so there was nothing already in place for follow-up with new Christians.

In the wee hours of the morning, driving back to their Altadena home, Dorothy finally broke the silence. "God has given us a huge home. Why don't we organize and host a Bible study class? We can cater a sit-down dinner, we have many friends who are well-known teachers and musicians, and we know of people we can invite as special guests to give their testimonies."

Lionel had been thinking the same thing, and wondering how they could add one more thing to their already-full plate of commitments. "Oh, Dorothy, God truly has given me one-of-a-kind partner," he said. "I don't even have to mention what I'm thinking. You're already there. I'm so grateful for the gift of you in my life."

Fifty-five new converts needed a Bible study. Lionel and Dorothy had the home that could accommodate it, the faith to believe for it, and the friends who could teach it. That's what they could see at the time. But God's vision is always so much bigger than ours.

Decision cards for those who made professions of faith that night at the LeTourneau meeting had not been obtained, so names were taken on scraps of paper or whatever was available.

Somehow, twenty of the fifty-five names were lost. Still enthused about the idea of a follow-up Bible study, Lionel and Dorothy went to a stationary store and picked out engraved invitations, personally addressed and prayed over each one, and sent them via special delivery to each of the thirty-five new believers. They prayed through their extensive list of connections for just the right person to lead the study, and felt led to call upon Charles Woodbridge of Fuller Seminary. The details came together, and the Bible study was set for Thursday evenings in their home.

The first week, only seventeen people came. The next week, attendance dropped to twelve. But as the word spread, the Bible study grew rapidly until the average weekly attendance reached two hundred and fifty. No longer able to accommodate the crowd inside, they moved the Bible study to the garden, but this was not conducive. The people were distracted by the scenery, and the neighbors objected to the loud speaker. They needed another solution.

As the last person walked down the front walk after the evening's gathering, Lionel told Dorothy, "Our home is too small. It just won't hold the Bible class. I'll get on the phone in the morning. We'll move the front wall and add five hundred square feet to the living room before next Thursday."

Dorothy swallowed, but she had been married too long to Lionel to object. She knew that if he wanted to enlarge the living room in a week, he would. And he did. The next morning, he ordered all workmen from his apartment projects to come up, and in one week they tore out the front of the house and extended the living room several hundred square feet so they could accommodate two hundred and fifty people in the Bible study class.

Lionel always did things in a big way, and he always had a great vision for what could be. When it came to developing people into their God-sized potential, he never believed any idea too small or any task too large. "When God is at the helm, nothing can stay the same," he would say. And just like in business, when he saw a need, he never looked at the monumental size; he only saw it as potential of what God could do.

That first year, more than five thousand people attended the Bible study in Lionel and Dorothy's Altadena home. No doctrinal differences were ever discussed. Only the gospel of the Lord Jesus Christ was presented. In addition to Charles Woodbridge, other teachers included Chester Paggett of the Bible Institute of Los Angeles and J. Edwin Orr, professor at the School of World Missions at Fuller Seminary and one of the greatest authorities in religious revivals in the Protestant world. They also brought in David Morken from Youth for Christ. Peak attendance would reach four hundred when Jack Wyrtzen and George Beverly Shea were brought in to speak and sing.

A typical Bible study session consisted of a brief song service, a special musical number, striking testimonies of businessmen and movie stars who had accepted Christ, a Bible lesson, and then catered refreshments. Afterward, the younger people would go swimming in the pool. No offering was taken. Lionel and Dorothy covered all expenses, including Scofield Bibles and a host of pamphlets and tracts that were given to those who needed them.

Not everyone who came to the class was saved, and not everyone who made a profession stood true. But God was definitely working. There were newcomers at every meeting, and Dorothy and Lionel saw many families repaired and suicidal people give their hopelessness to the God of all hope. Weekly, they would pick out a family, pray for them specifically, and invite them to the Bible study. The greatest satisfaction they had was seeing people come to know the Lord Jesus Christ.

The more Lionel and Dorothy witnessed God at work, the more their passion and faith ignited to dream bigger dreams for introducing others to Christ. Before long, the ministry of the Bible class spread to five sites—every city where Mayell Enterprises had a construction project. Charles Woodbridge resigned his position at Fuller Seminary, and Lionel retained him at a salary of $20,000 per year to be the full-time Bible study teacher, counselor, and chaplain for Mayell Enterprises employees, flying him weekly to each city to mentor workers and teach the Word of God.

On Monday nights, Charles Woodbridge flew to Tucson, Arizona, where he held noon Bible classes on the job for Mayell workers, then another Bible class in a home in the evenings. On Tuesdays, he traveled to Phoenix, where again he held noon classes for the workers and an evening class in a home that had facilities for 175 people. Wednesday meetings were held in a church in La Jolla, California, and on Thursdays he returned to teach the class in the Mayell home in Altadena. On Fridays, a class was held in the Santa Barbara home of John Strong, author and publisher of *Strong's Concordance*, where about one hundred people attended regularly.

Frequently, Lionel would bring in well-known Christians to give encouragement and share their testimony before the Bible studies, people like Roy Rogers and Dale Evans, Torrey Johnson, Billy Graham, George Beverly Shea, Cliff Barrows, and others. For all his workers who attended the noon classes, Lionel provided a catered lunch and paid them time-and-a-half wages.

The impact, even by today's standards, was phenomenal. Over a period of six years, gross attendance at the Mayell Enterprises Bible studies was estimated at over fifty thousand people. Thousands invited the Lord Jesus Christ into their lives. In 1958, *Moody Monthly* and other magazines published the story, and the success of the Bible studies became well known across the country. Billy Graham said that they were the finest he knew of, and his biography even tells of God's working in the Bible studies.

———

From small beginnings often come great things. A seed planted with a young couple who had a heart for youth became a worldwide ministry. A passion for reaching their city for Christ became an outreach to thousands. A Bible study that began with only seventeen new believers mushroomed into over fifty thousand people reached by the gospel of Jesus Christ.

The stories of lives changed would fill a library of books. Mom and Dad were available to be used by God to accomplish extraordinary things. Their vision wasn't about what *they* could do; it was about what *God* could do through them.

Mayell Enterprises Bible study for workers, Dr. Charles Woodbridge

Mom and Dad at his mother Una's grave, Forrest Lawn, 1948

AND THEN THERE WERE FIVE

THE SIRENS CAME TO a screeching halt, and the attendants rushed the patient from the ambulance into the
emergency room. But this patient was not just anyone. It was
Dorothy, Lionel's Rosebud, his life partner.

At home, she had experienced a deep stabbing pain and
become dizzy. Lionel heard a gasp and found his wife hugging
the door facing to keep from collapsing. He immediately called
the operator and requested an ambulance, which he then followed to the hospital, driving as skillfully as a race-car driver
down the busy Southern California streets.

He skidded into the closest parking space and burst through
the doors into the emergency room just as Dorothy was wheeled
in. She was now soaked with blood and in intense pain. At that
moment, nothing else mattered. Not their seven homes. Not the
building empire in four states. This was his Rosebud.

The doctors and nurses assured him she was in good hands, and Lionel moved back into the waiting room. He watched the hospital clock move slowly to the 6:30-p.m. mark. Minutes seemed like hours. What was taking so long? Thank God that Vince and Myrna, both adults and married, were watching their younger sister, eight-year-old Dottie, back home in Altadena.

Lionel borrowed the ER's telephone and called several Youth for Christ and CBMC friends to pray, along with his pastor, Henry Hutchins from Lake Avenue Congregational Church, where he and Dorothy were now actively involved. He had never experienced a medical emergency like this, and he paced the floor of the hospital, wracked with fear and anxiety. Only one word came to his mind: Jesus.

"Jesus! Jesus!" he cried out. "I have given you my business, my marriage, my life. Where are you? What are you doing?"

Just then, the doctor approached. He had a concerned look on his face, and Lionel's heart sank. "Mr. Mayell, Dorothy has a tubal pregnancy and she will lose another child, but that is not the only issue we uncovered. Her fertilized egg could not grow in the uterus because of a mass we uncovered. We did a needle biopsy, and it is cancer. Dorothy is in very serious condition."

The words pierced his heart like an arrow. This was not what he had expected to hear. Dorothy had previously lost a child, and he had feared that this might be the second. But Dorothy in serious condition? Cancer?

"What's next?" he managed to say through his tears.

"Only a miracle, Mr. Mayell. Only a miracle. She's way too weak for anything tonight. I would suggest not doing a thing right now. But we need to decide how and when it's safe to remove the mass. We're watching her closely, but she's lost a lot of blood. We're doing everything we can. You need to go home and get some rest."

Lionel had no words except the name of Jesus. He had nothing left emotionally and was numb spiritually. Slumped into a stiff emergency room chair, heartbroken, he cried out, "Jesus!"

Dr. Anderson, a family friend, and Dr. Jacobson, the family's physician, arrived to find Lionel slouched over in the chair. Neither said a word; their presence said it all. Dr. Anderson finally took Lionel's hand and said, "He has her, Lionel. He has this."

Lionel could not sit any longer. He went in to see Dorothy. She was groggy from the medication, and seeing her connected to IVs was unsettling. He kissed her on the forehead and assured her of his presence and love, then slipped out quietly. He needed to get some fresh air.

He got in the car and started to drive. He was not ready to go home but didn't know where to go. Soon he came upon an Assembly of God church that appeared to still be open. He had never been in one of these, but he immediately felt God's presence as he stepped into the back pew and knelt. He had nothing to say but the name of Jesus. The more he uttered His name, the more peace he felt. For a long time, he just listened for any word from his heavenly Father. No words came, but a kind of peace that passed his human understanding washed over him.

At that moment, he recognized the sense of peace described in Philippians 4:6–7: "In everything by prayer and supplication with thanksgiving let your requests be made known to God. And the peace of God, which surpasses all understanding, will guard your hearts and your minds in Christ Jesus" (ESV).

The Lord was near, and for the first time in hours, he felt assured that somehow Dorothy would be okay. Something in his heart had changed. God had exchanged his fear for peace. The sense he discerned was so strong, it was almost gravitational.

Lionel glanced at his watch. It was midnight. He bypassed the hospital and went home to his children. Little Dottie was sound asleep.

Vince met him at the door. "Dad, what happened? What happened at midnight?"

"Son, what do you mean?" he asked. "I don't know."

"I felt something at the time the grandfather clock chimed twelve. I was hoping you knew something."

Lionel shook his head. "No, I don't know anything, but I believe God has the answer."

At that moment, the phone rang. Lionel tripped over Vince as both rushed to pick up the receiver.

"Is this Mr. Mayell?" a man asked.

"Yes. Who is this?"

"This is Dr. Katz. I'm the doctor on duty, and I need to ask permission to x-ray your wife."

"What do you need an x-ray for?" Lionel asked. "She's been through enough."

"Mr. Mayell, something unexplainable has happened. The night nurse was making her rounds around eleven thirty and noticed that your wife looked different. Her coloring was back to normal, her vital signs were all back to normal, and she awakened and asked to go home. When the nurse checked your wife, she noticed that the bleeding had completely stopped. She called me. After studying her charts, I can't explain this either. But the mass appears to be gone. I can't feel it. I called in two other attending physicians who also gave Mrs. Mayell a complete checkup, and they too could not find the mass. After the loss of your little one, the mass was easily felt this afternoon, but now nothing. I'm requesting permission to do an x-ray."

Lionel was stunned. "Did you notice what time it was?" he stammered.

"Time? Yes, the time. I recorded it. It was twelve o'clock sharp."

The exact time Lionel was praying in the church. The exact time he had felt a sense of unexplainable peace. And the exact time Vince "felt something."

Lionel gave permission for the x-ray, and Vince and Lionel rushed back to the hospital. By the time they arrived, there was quite the commotion outside Dorothy's room. Dorothy was propped up in bed, alert, and she called out to Lionel, "I'm over here, honey."

That evening, tests confirmed that God had indeed miraculously healed Dorothy. The cancerous tumor detected earlier was no longer there. Bloodwork and x-rays were compared, and there was no sign of infection or tumor anywhere. Doctors could not find any scientific reason; it had been a miracle.

Later that week, Dorothy was examined by her regular OB/GYN. He strongly suggested that she and Lionel not try to have more children. Her body had been through too much, and he was concerned about complications if she were to become pregnant again. But Lionel and Dorothy knew that God had their future, and had proven His love and faithfulness concerning their hearts' desire for more children.

They continued with their busy lives, building own-your-own apartment projects in four states, hosting Bible studies in several cities, and investing in numerous ministries and God's dreams for others. Two years later, in 1955, God blessed them with a beautiful baby boy, Charles Carmen. Twenty-two months after that, daughter Ritalynn (the author) was born.

Never once during Dorothy's last two pregnancies did she experience nausea or any kind of complications. In fact, she was so healthy and they stayed so busy traveling that few acquaintances even realized she was pregnant until she showed up with a new baby. While seven months pregnant with Ritalynn, Dorothy was water skiing in Florida and riding roller coasters at Disneyland.

———

Dad was sixty years old when I was born as the youngest of five children, and Mom was thirty-nine. By the time I arrived, they had already lived a rather full and exciting life, and I was born at the peak of Dad's success as a builder and developer. He and Mom traveled extensively with his business, and since I was too young, I was usually left in the care of our governess (an exchange student from Sweden); our housekeeper, Melisha Jones; and our German Shepherd, Patsy. Sometimes Carmen was with us, but most of the time he was with Mom and Dad.

I can honestly say I don't remember my parents being gone a lot, but judging from the many letters and postcards in my baby book, they were. I developed a special bond with Melisha, and she became like my second mother. I loved my "Meshe," as I called her, and many of my fondest and earliest memories involve her, like the first time she took me to her church.

"Lionel," Mom said, "I still don't think this is a good idea. She can't sit still for one minute. She isn't Dottie." She had dressed me up in my crinoline outfit, white patent shoes, and little purse to match.

"Mother darling, this is good for her," Dad said. "Remember, Melisha's church doesn't stay seated for long like ours. Melisha knows exactly how to care for our Ritalynn."

I didn't understand what they meant, but it didn't matter. I was going to church with Meshe, and I could hardly wait. I jumped into our white 1957 Cadillac with Mom to make the trip across town.

"Now, Ritalynn," Mom cautioned, "you're a young lady, and young ladies do not squirm in church. They sit still and don't talk unless talked to, and whatever you do, don't chew gum. Remember, you are representing our family."

I don't think I truly heard one thing Mom said. I was going to Meshe's, and I loved her and her daughter, Mary. Mary was studying to be a nurse and sometimes came and took Meshe's place at night so Melisha could attend to her own family. (For years, I didn't know that Dad had paid for Mary's education and all Meshe's other children's schooling as well.)

I knew we were close when our Cadillac bounced over the railroad tracks and the scenery changed. We pulled in to the driveway of a nice white one-story home with a chain-link fence, and there was Mr. Jones all dressed up in his suit and hat, and Mary and Melisha in their white suits and hats. The other three children were dressed like me.

Mom greeted everyone with a hug and gave each child a gift, then spoke privately with Melisha for a few minutes. We all piled into Meshe's big brown station wagon, and I sat on Mary's lap with a big smile on my face as we bounced along on the potholed street to the Baptist church about two blocks away.

There, Melisha proudly led me inside and to her row, the third one on the right. I was not more than three feet tall and could not see anything over the large plumed hats in front. Meshe lifted me up and placed me on the wooden bench, then sang with all her heart and soul with her arms raised high. I just beamed at her. I loved her voice and I loved her.

The women were all dressed in white suits with hats and stiletto heels, while the men were dressed in three-piece suits and wearing hats. The large windows were open from the top, and big fans were blowing and the music was loud. The women all reached into their deep purses and pulled out tambourines and started to tap them. That made me giggle and clap, and Meshe hugged me closer. I could do no wrong.

During the message, people would say things like "amen," "preach it," "that's right," and "ah-hum, yes." Then the pastor must have said something particularly good because men and women threw handkerchiefs. I giggled until Meshe gave me a look. The service lasted a long time, and afterward people gathered for "Sunday dinner" in the basement. Unlike my parents' church, Meshe's church was like a party.

Years later, Meshe shared with me this next story, which took place when I was around two years of age:

> Ritalynn, you were your daddy's pride and joy. He carried you around like his treasure, his princess. And you did not like sharing him with anyone. You were spoiled, but as your dad would say, "She was born to be spoiled." I would tell your daddy, "Oh, Mr. Mayell, don't tell that child that. You'll be sorry. She is such a sweet little thing, but oh Mr. Mayell, don't tell her that."

You were living in Altadena, and your daddy was the president of CBMC in Pasadena, and he had a speaking engagement one evening. You had decided that your daddy should not go. You were a pistol. I kept telling you, "Honey, Daddy will be home soon." But you pursed your lips and went into the bathroom. All I heard a few minutes later was a flush of the toilet and your little giggle, "Tee-hee."

When I walked into the bathroom, I didn't notice anything wrong, but I saw mischief in your eyes. You were so proud of yourself, and you pointed to an empty soaking glass that had held your daddy's false teeth. "Oh no, Ritalynn, you did not!" You ran out of the bathroom, giggling, into your daddy's arms. I just knew you were going to get a paddling, and my heart was hurting. But when I told your daddy, he just picked you up in his arms and nuzzled his face into your chubby pink cheeks and said, "Ritalynn, Daddy loves his princess. I will be back soon." And he kissed you goodbye. His dentist was also a friend, and he had a spare pair in his office, which he opened for your dad.

From a very early age, I felt a special connection with my dad. Maybe it was because I looked so much like him. I was his spitting image—big dimples, blue eyes, square jaw, bright smile, boundless energy, and small stature. Or maybe it was because I was the baby of the family, but I think he felt it too. While I don't remember the false teeth story, I do recall, even at two years old, how I always wanted to be with my dad, how special he made me feel, and how he made everything an adventure.

Even something as mundane as cutting up fruit and making sandwiches:

I ran into the kitchen where Daddy was helping Melisha and Mom prepare for the Bible study guests. Daddy was wearing an apron, and Mom had made sure Meshe dressed me in crinolines and patent shoes, and brushed my hair. Standing on my tippy toes to get a better view of Daddy, I grunted loud enough to make sure he knew I was there.

Daddy picked me up. "There's my little princess. Sit right on the counter while Daddy cuts up the fruit."

"Daddy, will you make flowers for me?" I asked.

Being quite artistic, he began to cut roses out of strawberries, flowers out of cantaloupe pieces, and zig-zag handles out of the watermelon. Occasionally, my little fingers would grab a piece of fruit.

"Lionel, don't let Ritalynn do that. It's for the guests," Mom said.

"Oh, darling, her hands are sweet and won't do any harm. Look at these sweet hands! Jesus made these just for me to squeeze and kiss." He picked up my hands, then nuzzled them with his face, and kissed them all over.

"Oh, Lionel, she has you wrapped around her finger."

"Uh-huh, Mr. Mayell," Melisha agreed. "There's trouble in the makin'."

"Yes, she does have me, but God has her." When Daddy finished, his art had become a picnic basket with a handle and beautiful flowers cut from fruit. It was a masterpiece.

Clapping, I squealed, "Daddy, it is be-ute-ful!"

Next came the sandwiches. Mom had made chicken salad, egg salad, and homemade pimento cheese sandwiches. When she was not looking, I took my index finger and brushed the top of the bowl. Before I could make a half circle, she gave me a gentle tap on the finger.

"No, honey, please don't do that. You get away with this with your daddy, but not with me."

Daddy came and whisked me from the counter over to where he was making his favorite childhood sandwiches: cucumber, lettuce, and mayo. They were my favorite too. "Ritalynn, watch Daddy turn these sandwiches into something special."

"Yes, Daddy, yes. Hurry, hurry, Daddy." Any hurt feelings from Mom quickly vanished as I intently watched him. Everything she cooked was delicious, but Daddy was the artist. I giggled and laughed and clapped. He took the homemade breads Mom had made—sourdough, rye, wheat, and white—and placed them perfectly on top of the clean tile countertops.

"Um, I don't know what to do," he said. "Ritalynn, what color of bread should I use for this?" He pointed to the pimento cheese.

"White, Daddy, white," I replied.

He made everything fun. Meticulously, he took assorted breads and stuffed them with chicken salad, egg salad, or cucumber. I clapped and squealed.

"Now watch Daddy make these sandwiches change into a piece of art!" he said.

I leaned in to watch his every move. He cut the edges off the bread with a sharp knife and, with a wink, made sure they fell into my fingers. I stuffed my little face with cucumber and lettuce and giggled as I watched.

Mom was busy arranging her flower centerpieces on the tables, and every once in a while she stole a glance toward us, shook her head, and smiled. Nothing got past her. She knew Daddy and encouraged our relationship, although at times she tried to teach me manners. But I was not ready to be trained. I wanted to play. Many times, that's exactly what we did.

I loved being close to my daddy, and he would never let me be too far away either. As soon as I knew he was in the kitchen, I would stop whatever I was doing, run in, and stand and grunt to get his attention. There I stood, every little bit of less than three feet, with my gray-blue eyes and pursed lips.

We had this playful ritual going on. Daddy acted like he did not know I was standing there, and he and Mom would just continue to talk and sing. Suddenly, Mom would turn around and teasingly scare me and pretend to chase me. I would scream and run through the house. Meshe would just shake her head and smile. Then Mom would catch me, pick me up, and take me over to Daddy, whose arms were outstretched.

It seemed like we were always entertaining people, whether it was the Thursday night Bible study, guests for Dad's business, or a family who needed a home-cooked meal. Mom and Dad were always working together in the kitchen, cooking and laughing and enjoying each other. For larger crowds, Dad would pick up prepared food from the farmers' market at 3rd and Fairfax in Los Angeles, and they would add their touch with homemade salads, breads, and desserts. They were a team, we were a family, and their love was infectious.

Whenever the doorbell rang, Dad would whisk me up in his arms and carry me to the door to greet the guests. Often, they would hug Dad and then try to grab me from his arms. I am not sure who resisted more—me or him. I clung to his neck and refused to be pulled from his strong arms. When he felt my cling, he held me tighter. I was safe and secure in his love. I was his little princess, his living doll. He was proud to be my father, and he absolutely adored me and let me know it.

When I was two years old, we moved from our home in Altadena, California, to Florida. Dad was starting new developments in Palm Beach, Winter Park, and St. Petersburg. In the very beginning, we lived in the Alabama Hotel in Winter Park. Just as in California, Dad made every day an adventure.

"Ritalynn, do you want to go with Daddy to the office?" he asked one morning.

It did not matter where I was, I was ready to go. Mom told me one time I even jumped out of the bathtub to go. Daddy's office was located on one of the numerous Winter Park lakes, so to get to work he drove our speedboat across the lake. I loved the water and, even more, I loved to go fast. Sometimes I would sit on Daddy's lap and steer the boat as he would make loud engine noises. I would giggle and laugh, believing I was the one driving.

Even though Daddy was a successful businessman and busy with mission work, he always took time to be with me and my brother. Sometimes Carmen would join us, but most of the time it was just Daddy and me.

By the time I was four, Mom and Dad had purchased a home on the Intracoastal Waterway in St. Petersburg. Early on Saturday mornings, we would drive to the shipyards and train docks that delivered fresh fruit from all over the States. Truck drivers would pull up and unload their rigs while we drove alongside, deciding what produce to view.

Then Daddy would swerve to one side of the road, stop the car, and jump out. "Ritalynn, sweetheart, I think I've struck gold!"

My little fingers would open the door and leave it wide open as I ran to where he was looking into a huge crate. Picking up a large cantaloupe, he smelled the fruit and then leaned over to let me copy him.

"It smells good, Daddy, doesn't it?" I said, imitating him.

He smiled and took my hand in his as he thumped the cantaloupe and mashed his finger on the top, explaining why this one was not ripe enough or why that one was just perfect. He asked the guy to cut it open and let us taste. As the man took a big knife out, Daddy squeezed my hand and winked. I loved how he took every opportunity to teach and was never bothered with my curious questions.

With our car loaded full of fresh fruits and vegetables and our bellies full, we started for home. Even driving home was an adventure. He made it a game by never going the same way. "Ritalynn, should Daddy turn this way or that way?"

As I squealed with delight and pointed, he turned in that direction, making siren sounds and exaggerating each turn. I giggled and screamed even more. I loved that I could be as loud as I wanted.

When we arrived home and unloaded our car, Daddy sat me on the countertop so I could watch as he peeled and chopped the assorted fruit for breakfast. We always ate breakfast on the glassed-in porch facing the Intracoastal, where we could watch for dolphin fins.

I anticipated what came next—fishing. Daddy would retrieve our fishing poles from the garage, and Carmen and I followed him to our boat dock, where the bucket of live shrimp bait dangled in the salt water. I liked fishing with Daddy, even though it was hard not to talk. Standing as close as possible to him, I gazed up with a big smile and then suddenly felt a tug on my pole. I smacked Daddy on the arm and pointed, being careful not to make a sound.

"Good, Ritalynn," he encouraged me. "Reel it in! You have a big one!"

Carmen clapped and squealed, and Mom came running out of the house with her camera. It turned out to be a blow fish, and when it came out of the water, it puffed up like a balloon.

"Quick, Ritalynn!" Mom screamed. "Get it back into the water. It is going to pop, honey!"

Laughing as he took my pole, Daddy released the fish back into the water and then hugged me as if to say, "It's all right, honey. There'll be another fish."

He seemed to know me best. He knew when I was disappointed, and he knew the sincerity of my heart when others thought I was too young to be taken seriously. We regularly attended First Baptist Church in St. Petersburg, and I was only four years old when a visiting young evangelist with Youth for Christ came and preached. That night I decided to invite Jesus Christ into my heart as my personal Savior. I remember it vividly, and even at my young age, I knew exactly what I was doing.

As Mom was trying to make sure I understood my decision, Carmen reached for my hand. "I want to take her down front," he said.

I still remember the ahhs as my brother and I held hands and walked toward the front. Daddy was standing close by, and after the pastor talked with me, he came over and picked me up and hugged me close. Daddy's little princess, secure in his arms.

———

All of these experiences modeled to me the love of my Father God and how He, too, longs to lavish upon us. Dad's love carried far greater impact than I ever realized. It gave me value and honor in who I was. It gave me a self-confidence to try new things and to risk making decisions when others thought I was too young, and the courage to explore and to ask questions when I did not understand.

A powerful bond was built during my early years—a bond of trust that later transferred to my heavenly Father. Dad became a safe place where I would always feel free to run and know I was accepted just as I was.

Dad and me, 1958

Family of five: L to R me, Mom, Dottie, Dad, Carmen

MENTORING A MURDERER

DOROTHY WAS DRIVING BACK to Lionel's office in St. Petersburg with her car full of office supplies when the radio announcer broke in, "We interrupt our broadcast to bring you the latest national news. Dennis Whitney, the seventeen-year-old serial killer apprehended by police last month in Palm Beach County, was convicted and sentenced to death by electric chair this afternoon by a Miami jury."

Dennis Whitney had viciously murdered six men, most of whom were gas station attendants, and violently bludgeoned one woman to death after abducting her from a Sears parking lot. According to the announcer, he would become the young-est death-row inmate at Raiford Prison (now known as Union Correctional Institution). The announcer continued, "Whitney began smoking at age eight and drinking at ten. By age twelve, he was a veteran of several armed robberies, and five years later, in 1960, he launched a cross-country murder spree, notching the handle of his stolen .22-caliber pistol for each of the seven victims he killed between California and Florida."

People all throughout downtown St. Petersburg honked their horns to celebrate Whitney's conviction. Prior to his capture, residents along the central Florida coast had lived in fear when he had been spotted in the immediate area. But instead of feeling joy over his conviction, Dorothy's heart was burdened for the young man. She sped toward the Whispering Waters project office in St. Petersburg.

"Lionel!" Dorothy was out of breath with excitement when she entered the office. "Where are you?"

Lionel came to meet her. "Darling, is something wrong?"

"No, but yes, honey. Do you remember when we were driving from California a few months ago? We were in New Mexico when we heard on the radio that a service-station attendant had been murdered by being shot in the back of the neck? The next day, another murder occurred, another attendant at a service station. They began to talk on the radio about a conspiracy across the country, and no one knew who would be next. People were terrified.

"Then last month in Palm Beach County, down the street from your new development, another gas station attendant was shot. And then a woman was killed. They finally caught the killer, a young red-haired teenager. Well, today that young man was sentenced to execution by electric chair.

"Daddy, you have to go down to the jail where he's being kept before they transfer him to Raiford Prison. Not just anyone will have access to him, but you can use your influence to help this kid know Jesus. You're a father. You know the Lord Jesus Christ, and you must give him an opportunity to know that God loves Him. Jesus paid for his sins too, even as horrible as they are. Daddy, you must go."

Lionel wasn't sure why she was so moved by Dennis Whitney's story, but he knew that her sense of spiritual discernment was usually right. He needed to go. "Darling, I will," he said.

He got on the phone with his attorneys, asking if they would arrange with the Palm Beach Police for him to see Dennis Whitney, and days later, he made the five-hour drive across Florida to Palm Beach. He was given one hour.

Guards escorted a scared, angry teenager, his feet and hands bound in chains, into the room. Dennis slumped into the metal chair and faced Lionel, his expression blank.

Lionel was not intimidated. He looked into Dennis's eyes and, after introducing himself, got to the heart of why he was there. There was no time to waste. "Dennis, I don't know your upbringing, but I'm certain anyone who could commit the crimes you've committed, was never loved. I'm here to tell you that there is someone who does love you, and to whom you can belong. This person is Jesus Christ, who died in your place on a cross for everything you ever did wrong, so you can have a clear record with God forever. He loves you.

"You're at the end of yourself. You just turned seventeen, and you've admitted that there isn't much you haven't done in your short lifetime. Will you say this simple prayer with me? 'Dear Lord, I want to accept Jesus Christ as my Savior, and thank Him from the bottom of my heart for forgiving me of all my sins.'"

Dennis remained unmoved, almost defiant. "Mr. Mayell, I won't lie to you. I don't know if Jesus Christ is the Son of God. I don't know if he's my Savior, and if He really died for me. I certainly wouldn't bow my head to Him. I don't believe He would want to be my Savior, so I won't tell him I want him to be my Savior and forgive my sins and place the blood over my sins and the sins of the whole world. That's just stupid."

Lionel tried again. "Will you do this? You don't have to bow your head if you don't want to. Why don't you say, 'Dear Lord, dear God.' If there is a God, He can hear this conversation right now. If I'm right, why would you miss out on the greatest free gift? What could you possibly lose?"

Dennis shrugged. Then awkwardly and almost childlike, he began speaking, nearly shouting, as if God needed help hearing. "Dear God, I believe there is a God. I hope so anyway. I'm asking you—no, I don't ask, I tell you—get into my heart and cover me with your blood and save me. *If* Jesus Christ is your Son, will you prove it to me? I don't know nothing about religion, but I want to know what it is to be saved. Most of all, I don't know what it means to know love."

Lionel restrained himself to keep from grabbing Dennis and hugging him, but he knew that every officer in the room would have intervened. Dennis was just a scared kid who had never been loved or cared about. Lionel asked the guards if he could shake Dennis's hand, but he was not allowed to touch him.

Lionel left the jail a changed man that day. He had gone to encourage a serial killer, but instead he had received a gift that would alter his future forever. One month later, Dennis Whitney was moved to Raiford Prison in Starke, Florida, about three and a half hours from St. Petersburg, and placed on death row.

Four months later, in the spring of 1961, Lionel received his first of two dozen letters from Dennis Whitney:

Dear Lionel,

I want you to know that God has revealed to me that Jesus Christ is His Son and He is my Savior. Thank you for introducing me to Him. I am different. I knew there was a God because why would anyone take time to visit me and love me as you if there was not something greater that moved upon them to do so. You are a true friend. My mother was a prostitute and my dad an alcoholic. I was beaten all the time as a kid. My parents told me I was a mistake and a worthless piece of junk. I left home when I was ten. I don't have anyone and I have no idea where the rest of my brothers and sisters are, and even if I did they would probably be too embarrassed to visit. Will you come and visit me? The warden will have to send you the invite.

I want to know Jesus better. Thank you.

Your friend and now brother in Jesus Christ,
Dennis Whitney
000000001, Raiford Prison, 1961

Lionel could hardly wait for the invitation from the warden. A few days later, he arrived at Raiford Prison and was escorted into a large room where prisoners were cordoned off in what resembled telephone booths of two-inch-thick plate glass. Seated in one booth, on the opposite side of the glass fitted with an intercom, was Dennis Whitney.

Lionel was shocked by change in Dennis's appearance. The expression on his face was winsome instead of hardened, his features had softened, and his personality was engaging. He had a big smile on his face, his eyes were clear, and he began talking before Lionel could even sit down. Dennis was no longer sullen; instead, he seemed like an excited child sharing with his parent. Lionel had never seen such a change in a human being; they had a lot to catch up on. Visits were limited to twenty minutes at Raiford, so Lionel had driven over three hours one way for less than a half-hour visit.

For the next two years, Lionel made the seven-hour round trip to Raiford Prison to visit with Dennis twice a week, encouraging him and teaching him the Bible during their limited time together. He wrote Dennis three one-page single-spaced letters (prison regulations) each week. When Lionel was traveling on business and unable to make the trip, Dorothy would write the letters and visit Dennis, bringing him homemade goodies when she came. Of course, every letter was opened and stamped "Censored" by prison officials, and every food item closely scrutinized. Lionel sent Dennis a Bible and other Christian books to read, including a biography signed by Billy Graham and addressed personally to Dennis. After a few months, all the guards welcomed Lionel and looked forward to his visits.

Dennis wrote Lionel frequently, and in his letters, he told of other inmates on death row who came to know the Lord through the Bibles and books that Lionel had sent. At the time, death-row inmates were allowed no television, very little reading material, and only a transistor radio that was shared by several inmates. Hardened criminals were so desperate that they begged to read

Dennis's books and letters. Some inmates, when they found out the letters and books were religious, mocked him.

One prisoner asked to read Dennis's signed biography from Billy Graham and as a result came to accept Christ as his Savior. In Dennis's letters to Lionel, he told of the books being traded among the death-row inmates as if they were the most valuable treasures.

Almost two years to the day of their first meeting, as Lionel was leaving for one of his weekly visits with Dennis, he received a disturbing letter from the superintendent of the prison:

Dear Mr. Mayell:

Dennis Whitney has been enjoying your letters each week for the last year. Our warden is Catholic and has made arrangements for two Catholic sisters who live near Raiford to visit the prison frequently and to bring in fancy cookies and homemade goods they make in their own kitchens. They also pray with Dennis. It is therefore no longer necessary for you to commit to visiting or writing him any further. We are kindly asking for you to desist from all contact with Dennis Whitney.

Lionel was heartbroken and bewildered. Why would anyone who claimed to know Jesus ask him to stop contacting another believer? He was unable to contact Dennis to explain what happened, and received one last letter from Dennis in the fall of 1962:

Lionel,

I have not heard from you since you heard I was now a Catholic. I am sorry you are so mad and will no longer write to me or visit. I thought you loved me. I could never have an offense against you. You were the first to ever sincerely love me. Even though you were busy with business, had a family and other responsibilities, you took the time to drive over six hours round trip for twenty minutes. You paid for a new lawyer that you felt could help with my appeals to get off of death row and into life in prison. You believed in me and sent me books, answered my questions and even though prison restrictions prevented you from sending over a single-spaced page letter, you sent the max correspondence of three letters per week to answer my questions and encourage me. You hired investigators that tracked down two of my sisters and paid out of your pocket for them to visit me.

I will always love you and appreciate you most of all for having the courage and the heart to visit a seventeen-year-old who had violently murdered to tell him about Jesus. Thank you.

In His Grace,
Dennis Whitney,
000000001, Raiford Prison, November 1962

Lionel couldn't respond. Dennis never knew that Lionel had been asked to suspend all contact with him. As for Dennis, he was condemned to die for two 1960 murders and admitted to five other slayings. He spent twelve years on death row and came within two days of dying in the electric chair before his sentence was commuted to life in prison in 1972, when the U.S. Supreme Court declared Florida's death penalty law unconstitutional. He was moved off death row into a regular cell until his death of natural causes in 2005.

He had spent almost forty-four years in prison, but God had protected him from execution.

———

I contacted Raiford Prison and learned that in all the years in confinement, Dennis was never disciplined for behavior issues. This once desperate and most hopeless of sinners had been redeemed by the love of a Savior, and through him, countless others in prison came to know the love of Jesus Christ. How many prayers of parents and grandparents were answered during those forty-four years, we will never know, but the impact of Dad's first visit had a ripple effect for all eternity.

WHOSE VOICE DO I HEAR?

D AD'S BUSINESSES CONTINUED TO mushroom in California, Arizona, and Florida. He remained involved with CBMC while Mom served in Christian Women's Club, and together they served with Youth for Christ. My sister Dottie attended boarding school at Hampden Dubose Academy nearby in Zellwood, Florida, while Carmen and I enjoyed the nice things that success afforded: speedboats, sailing, and flying with Dad's best friend in his twin-engine plane.

Dad's accomplishments introduced him to key influencers in Florida, two of whom became close friends: Judge Jim Welch of Lakeland, Florida, and Walt Meloon, the creator and founder of Correct Craft, the premier sailboat, powerboat, and race-boat manufacturer based in Orlando. These men in turn introduced him to Torrey and Gordon Mosvold, sons of one of Norway's leading shipping and industrial magnates worth hundreds of millions of dollars. The brothers showed great interest in Dad's condominiums, and invited our entire family to Norway to meet their families and discuss their business proposition.

In the spring of 1961, Mother and Daddy boarded a plane for Norway, via the North Pole and Iceland, and landed in a sightseer's paradise. Carmen and I were too young for this voyage and stayed in the care of our governess from Sweden, Lena. In the postcards received from Norway, we learned of the instantaneous bond between the families and that a business deal had quickly been negotiated and signed.

After one month in Norway, Mother and Daddy returned home with a million dollars in investor funding to begin development of Whispering Waters in Palm Beach. They were elated. Mayell Enterprises had progressively grown into an established organization with nine companies, including Mayell Builders of Arizona, California, and Florida. The companies were all at their peak, but the cash was tied up in building projects. This new adventure was to develop land along the oceanfront in Palm Beach, near the famous Breakers Hotel.

As they had practiced for over twenty years in partnership together, they identified the property to purchase, acquired it in faith, and moved the family into our new Palm Beach waterfront home. Life seemed to be on track.

Then Daddy received a phone call: "Lionel, this is Bill Bright. I've called because I need your and Dorothy's assistance. We are expanding Campus Crusade for Christ into Rollins College in Winter Park, and since you have a home and a huge development there, I was wondering if you would consider financially supporting our new director for Rollins College and underwriting the expenses for expanding Campus Crusade's work at Rollins? Besides, Lionel, the director is a kid who needs someone like you and Dorothy to lean on for wisdom, guidance, and discernment."

"Bill, let me get Dorothy," he said. "I'm thinking we don't even have to pray about it. You know how we've always loved and supported the ministry of Campus Crusade. God has just blessed us with another new project in Palm Beach, which we will begin soon. Although we've moved to our new home in Palm Beach, we still have our home in Winter Park and will be back in that area frequently."

Mom joined the call, and without further discussion agreed with Dad. It was set. They committed on the spot to be the financial backers for the extended Campus Crusade work at Rollins. And why not? There were no red flags in their hearts, and it was, after all, God's work.

Within months of that decision, the fortunes of Mayell Enterprises shifted, and four of the five companies entered a period of serious financial difficulty. The unparalleled "favor" that Dad had experienced in his business since he became a Christian seemed in doubt. To this day, it is not clear what actually happened. All Dad would say was that some of the younger executives in his companies disagreed with Dad's philosophy and principles for running the business and decided to follow their own strategies. Only one company, The Samarkand in Santa Barbara, appeared to follow Dad's principles, exhibited sound management, and continued to turn a profit.

Daddy was devastated, his faith shaken. His business had been "attacked" before from outside the company, and he had always bounced back. But never had he experienced such issues within the company. Had God withdrawn his blessing from Mayell Enterprises, even after they had declared He was their business partner? Was God redirecting their steps? Was there another plan? How was he to interpret this? The questions swarmed in his head, but there were no answers.

With nowhere to turn, he and Mother fell to their knees and cried out to God, "We have given you the helm of this business as our sole partner for over twenty years. You've never failed us. If we saw a need in others or heard of their dreams from you, we stepped up and bridged the gap with every resource we could offer. We believe you are God and you are a rewarder of those who diligently seek you. Lord, we have been faithful to believe, but what is happening?"

They remained on their knees for some time, desperately seeking answers and reminding God of everything, big or little, they had done. They reminded Him of the Lord's Account, which had now increased from receiving 30 percent of their income to 60 percent. But answers never came. God seemed silent. And the fear inside grew.

Daddy called the Mosvold brothers the next day and canceled the business deal for Palm Beach. Then he called Bill Bright and gave up their lifelong dream to be involved in ministry with Bill and Vonette and the new venture at Rollins College. He and Mother were alone in this journey, in this challenge to their faith. The benefactor for others' dreams had no one to come alongside to mentor and encourage him to remain bold in his faith.

In the ensuing days and nights, the battle between fear and faith raged on. Many times, they cried themselves to sleep, rehearsing, "My Father is faithful. He is faithful." In his spirit, Daddy sensed that God was saying, "Trust Me. I'm doing something new." But fear would press in with questions that clouded his mind. What would happen if he no longer had money and success? Would his precious Dorothy divorce him?

At the same time, Mom sensed God was speaking to her with a message that would affirm His message to Daddy. "Dorothy, I have not withdrawn my blessing. It may look different, but I have you both." As she had done many times before, she spoke with the conviction of faith: "Lionel, God has our next steps. I am confident. We can trust God."

Mom wrote in her journal, "I knew I had heard God speak and I was scared to death of the new and how my life may change again. God reminded me of His faithfulness. I was committed to Lionel, our marriage, and most of all to the Lord Jesus Christ, which superseded anything else."

While the next step wasn't clear, one thing was certain: they would trust God and take it together.

Only a few days had passed when a phone call came from Theodora Heyne, a friend and influential member of the advisory board for Houston's bid to win the new NASA Manned Spacecraft Center. The year was 1961, and President John F. Kennedy had just set the goal for the Apollo Program to land men on the moon by the end of the decade. Politicians in nearly every major city were exerting political pressure to win the bid, as the new space center would become the heart of the largest scientific and engineering community in the country with combined projected salaries of more than $60 million a year.

Houston, because of its strategic location and proximity to a culturally attractive community, was a strong favorite of the site selection team. But it was the state's native son, Vice President Lyndon B. Johnson, plus other senior Texas congressmen who could exert significant political pressure on the final decision. To further differentiate the city's bid, Theodora Heyne wanted to include a proposal for upscale housing for the thousands of scientists and engineers who would be drawn to the "city within a city." They needed a well-known builder whose design and vision were at the forefront of "home ownership without the maintenance." Someone with the credentials and national reputation of Lionel Mayell.

Daddy was honored, humbled, and utterly excited. The decision on the Manned Spacecraft Center location was to be made in the next twenty days, and Theodora Heyne and the advisory board needed his answer within forty-eight hours.

This could be a great opportunity for Mayell Enterprises. Daddy had already been considering Houston as a potential for expansion of his own-your-own concept, and he had already been making regular trips to the city scouting for property and locations. On his most recent trip, he found the perfect property in the middle of what was known as Houston's "magic circle," less than thirty minutes from the site proposed for the Manned Spacecraft Center near Rice University. This could represent the crown jewel of his developments, and it was certainly no coincidence that he had already been considering Houston; God had placed the desire in his heart. Theodora Heyne said as much, and she was quite persuasive.

Still, Daddy needed to discuss the opportunity with Mom, and they needed to pray and hear directly from God. On the one hand, it seemed like this was an answer to prayer that would continue his same career path in building own-your-owns. Or was this the "something new" that he thought he heard the Lord speak of? After much prayer, they both knew by the peace in their hearts that Houston was the next step.

On September 19, 1961, eighteen days after Theodora Heyne's call, Houston won the bid for the NASA Manned Spacecraft Center, known today as the Lyndon B. Johnson Space Center.

Houston was a go.

EXTRAVAGANT LIFE, EXTRAVAGANT LOVE

I WAS ONLY FIVE WHEN our family moved from St. Petersburg to Houston in 1962. We never sold our homes when we moved to a new city, instead keeping them as a place to stay when Mom and Daddy traveled back for business, and using them for missionaries who needed temporary housing or evangelical leaders and speakers who needed the privacy and comfort of a personal home.

Our new home was in Tanglewood, a quiet upscale neighborhood in western Houston that was known for its large lots, stately oak trees, and clubby atmosphere. The sprawling one-story house with beautiful landscaping was our fifth home.

For Mom and Daddy, the business "scare" of the previous few months quickly faded as we got swept up in our busy new lives as part of Houston society. Daddy was planning the most ambitious of all his developments, the Ambassador at Post Oak, and was highly sought after for board positions. Mom worked alongside him as his partner in the business, became involved in the Christian Women's Club, and soon became its president. My sister Dottie had an "etiquette tutor" and was often featured in the society pages of the newspaper, and Carmen and I were enrolled in private Christian schools.

Our family was treated like American royalty. Daddy and Mom's pictures were frequently in the newspaper for some social or business function, and so were ours on occasion. We were invited to every grand opening and big event in town, recognized wherever we went, and never had to wait for tables in fine restaurants. Our family often received free trips in exchange for endorsements for a new restaurant, bed and breakfast, or guest ranch in the Texas Hill Country.

Life was always busy, and we lived it on a grand scale. We traveled on helicopters, on airplanes, and in private berths on passenger trains. When Daddy traveled for his developments in different states, we were taken out of school for months at a time so we could go along. Mom arranged with the principal and teachers for our classwork assignments ahead of time so we never fell behind in our studies.

It was subtle at first, almost imperceptible, but there was a different vibe to our new life in Houston. A sort of pressure to be always "on," with a lot more emphasis on how I looked, dressed, and acted. My clothing needed to be "approved" before I stepped out of the house, even if it was to play. My outfits were always perfectly matched.

We were schooled in the finer graces of Southern aristocracy, such as dressing for dinner and eating with sterling silver flatware and china at every meal. I was expected to curtsy when greeting adults, and Carmen had to bow from the waist. Daddy and Mother thought that important since we were often introduced to people like astronaut John Glenn and former president Dwight Eisenhower. Billy Graham stayed in our home, and we went to his home in North Carolina in the summer.

Mother and Daddy's life changed too. Before, they had been at the forefront of evangelism through parachurch groups like Campus Crusade for Christ, Young Life, and CBMC, and they thrived on the personal involvement and direct impact they had on changing lives. Daddy tried to start a local chapter of CBMC, but businessmen were not interested in joining something outside the church. Being in the Deep South was different. Here, things were centered around the church, and the church was all about status.

———

Our neighborhood, I came to learn, was all about status too. The residents prided themselves on living in a sophisticated, all-adult neighborhood, and frowned upon families with small children. Kids were noisy, messy, and had toys scattered about the front yard. These homeowners liked to keep their neighborhood exactly the way it was—pristine, quiet, exclusive, and uppity. I guess they made an exception for us because Daddy was the famous builder who was developing the prestigious Ambassador at Post Oak.

Because there were no other children my age in Tanglewood and church was thirty minutes away, Carmen was my best friend and only playmate. We needed somewhere to play at home out of sight of neighbors, so Daddy built a swimming pool and pool house in the backyard, and that became the focus of our summer activities. When we got loud, as kids do, sometimes the phone would ring, and it would be a neighbor complaining about the noise. Mom would try to shush us, but Daddy would just scream underwater to muffle the sound. Daddy stuck up for me as he always had.

Mom and Daddy did everything they could to make up for our not having playmates in the neighborhood. We had taffy pulls, played board games, cooked smores in the fireplace, and held mock evangelistic crusades in our living room. Dottie played the piano, I sang into a microphone, and Carmen preached sermons, sometimes for hours and hours. Often, late at night, Daddy would spontaneously pile us all in the car, still wearing our pajamas, for a trip to the drug store to get a nickel cone of ice cream. He would pretend to be a race-car driver, Mom would scream, and we kids would giggle with uncontrolled laughter.

I'm sure Daddy didn't have a lot of spare time; he was a prominent and highly successful businessman with companies in four states and dozens of important building projects coast to coast. Even so, he always *made* the time for us. It was his priority as a father. He made me feel important even as a child, like I was never too young to ask questions or make important decisions; what I thought or felt was never insignificant. He always believed me, and believed *in* me; he studied me and knew me before I even said a word. Each of us kids felt the same way. Countless stories that illustrate that, but I'll focus on a few that say it best for me.

———

Not long after we moved to Houston, I wanted to be baptized. I had received Christ in Florida the previous year, when I was four, but no one in the Houston area would baptize me because they thought I was too young. My mother was neutral on the subject, but Daddy recognized what was in my heart.

"Ritalynn, come here to Daddy," he said.

I dropped my doll and ran to his outstretched arms.

He lifted me onto his lap. "Tell Daddy why you want to be baptized."

"Daddy, I just do. It's what you are s'posed to do after asking Jesus into your heart." I squeezed Daddy's face and declared in my newly acquired Texas drawl, "And, Daddy, you just have to help me."

That was all it took. He stood from the chair with me still in his arms, walked into the kitchen, and grabbed the Rolodex card file with names and phone numbers. Placing me on top of the counter, he began to thumb through the hundreds of contacts.

Mom later filled in the gaps for me: "Ritalynn, your daddy was determined to get you baptized. He called key leaders he believed could have some influence. For hours, he contacted every church denomination where he knew people, and every ministry, but no one was helpful. But your daddy was determined. He called our former pastor in Florida where you accepted Christ. The pastor immediately said, 'Of course. I know Ritalynn made a decision for Christ and understand what she did. You just bring her to Florida.'"

Daddy slammed down the receiver after hearing that. "Praise the Lord! Mother, Carmen, I'm taking Ritalynn to Florida this weekend. She's going to be baptized."

Carmen helped me off the counter, and Mom cried as we all held hands and danced in a circle. I knew Daddy would fix it.

"Ritalynn, is there anyone else besides me who you want to go?"

"Carmen, Daddy," I said. "Carmen!"

A few days later, my brother, Dad, and I boarded a plane to Florida.

I was only about three and a half feet tall, and the church baptismal was about four and a half feet deep and nine feet wide. The water would be over my head, so I would have to swim to the pastor in the baptismal's center. Both the pastor and Daddy examined the situation while Carmen and I sat on the side steps and watched. I was sure Daddy would think up something that would make it safe for me.

The next thing I knew, Carmen and I were whisked off to the hardware store, where Daddy purchased two cinderblocks. He and the pastor placed them on the bottom of the empty baptismal, making stepping stones for me, then filled the baptismal. While Daddy held my hand, I tested walking down the steps onto the cinderblocks. It was perfect.

That Sunday evening, Daddy and Carmen sat in the front row. Barefoot and wearing my white T-shirt and shorts, I stepped into the baptismal and crossed the cinderblocks while the pastor held my hand. I was only five years old, but that day is as fresh in my mind as if it were today. The pastor's eyes kept me focused as he assisted me onto the second cinder block. He took such great care and was so tender with me. He explained to the congregation that I had accepted Christ in their church about a year ago during a message from a Youth for Christ speaker but was now living in Houston and had come back just to get baptized.

"Ritalynn, have you asked Jesus into your heart?" he asked.

"Yes sir, I have!" I shouted in my Texas accent.

Oohs and ahhs from the congregation filled the church auditorium.

"Do you know what baptism is?"

"Yes sir, I do. It's so y'all can see what Jesus has done for me!"

The people roared with laughter and clapped.

I looked from the pastor to my daddy. It was hard to see with the bright lights, but I spotted him sitting in the front row, wiping his eyes with his white handkerchief. Carmen held Daddy's hand, grinning from ear to ear.

The pastor covered my nose and mouth with a folded handkerchief, then ever so gently immersed me in the water. My feet came up off the cinderblock, and the pastor carried me to the opposite set of stairs where a lady was waiting for me with a towel.

Before she could dry me off, Daddy was there. He was always there. I couldn't understand how he got to where I was so fast. But I could always count on him to be there right when I needed him.

Now everyone would know that I too believed in Jesus.

———

I was a curious child, and my hunger for God started early. When I was around six years old, my family began attending the Berachah Church in Houston, pastored by Bob Thieme. It was the first time I had ever seen a pastor use an overhead projector to teach. He drew a circle and talked about the sovereignty of God, then drew another figure to illustrate that God never changed, another symbol to signify that God was all knowing, and continued with a list of God's attributes. I listened intently and took my crayons and tried to copy what I could from his illustrations.

Daddy must have noticed my struggle. The very next week, he brought a little black-and-white notebook and pencil home from his office. "Ritalynn, this is for you to take to church so you can write like a big adult. Would you like that?"

I grabbed my present. "Yes, Daddy, yes!"

The following week, we sat closer to the front and I spent the entire service copying the overhead projector notes. Although I did not really grasp the meaning, it piqued my interest and I wanted to know more. During Sunday supper after church, I peppered Mom and Daddy with incessant questions: "Can you tell me what 'soverty' [sovereignty] means? Why is it so 'portant' [important] that God can't change? Why ..."

Mom sneezed. "Ritalynn, you're making me nervous. Please, not now. Let us enjoy our dinner."

Undeterred, I kept asking questions.

"Ritalynn,"—Daddy cleared his throat while looking at Mom— "Daddy will make sure you understand and have all of your questions answered, okay?"

"Oh, Lionel, she has you wrapped around your finger," Mom said. "She's just being dramatic."

"No, I beg to differ. This time I don't think so. There's a deep need to know, and I want to encourage her and feed that hunger." Daddy knew me well, and he followed through on his promise the very next week in a big way.

"Ritalynn!" he called when he came home from work. "Daddy has a surprise for his princess."

I dashed into the living room, fully expecting to see a present. He had nothing in his hands.

"Ritalynn, tomorrow we're going to have lunch with Pastor Thieme, and he wants to answer your questions personally."

I ran into my bedroom and grabbed my notebook, then ran back and thrust it into his hands. "Daddy, I have lots of questions in there. Will he have time to give me every answer?"

Daddy smiled and picked me up. "If not, honey, we will make another appointment."

I was satisfied.

The next day I was dolled up in my best Sunday dress and perfectly pressed crinolines, with my permed Shirley Temple haircut with bangs cut straight across high above my brows. My little legs were stretched straight out on the back seat of our white Cadillac, and I clutched my black-and-white notebook to my chest.

Pastor Thieme greeted me as if I were an adult. I took out my notebook and pointed to the diagrams and asked him to explain every detail. He spent a long time with me, explaining his teaching on the sovereignty of God on the level I could understand, then remarked to Daddy that he wished his entire congregation would be this interested in his messages.

That day, Dad's encouragement and belief that I was not too young to understand more about God unleashed in me a hunger to know Him that has continued for decades.

———

Daddy encouraged my curiosity about spiritual things, but he was also there to help me when I struggled with other things. When I was in first grade, my teacher at Long Point Baptist Day School sent a note home expressing concern that I would not be able to move to second grade because my reading ability was well below average. Unbeknownst to me at the time, Daddy undertook a project to help me read, all the while making it seem like fun and games.

He called around and discovered that there was a book-mobile dispatched from the downtown Houston main library and it would be parked in a shopping center near our home all summer long. He decided to become my tutor, and made going to the bookmobile a father-daughter outing.

"Ritalynn, how would you like to go to the drug store and get a cherry Coke with a big scoop of vanilla ice cream?" he said. "Then Daddy has a big surprise for his little girl."

There was no need to say anything more. The promised ice cream and surprises were enough to get my full commitment.

While I slurped my cherry Coke and ice cream through a straw, he told me about his surprise. "We're going to visit a library on wheels."

"On wheels?" I kicked my legs on the front of the counter with excitement until he quietly tapped me so I would settle down.

"We're going to pick out some books that you would like to read, and Daddy is going to read with you every day."

I discovered that I loved biographies, and together we picked out books about George Washington Carver, Louisa May Alcott, and other underdogs who overcame obstacles. Then, every day without fail, Daddy sat for hours while I read aloud to him. When I got stuck on a word, he would help me sound out each syllable. I tended to want to get done quickly, so I would sometimes race through the text without understanding what I was reading. He would put his hand over the book and ask me to tell him what I just read. It took a while, but Dad was consistent and it slowed me down enough to think about what I was reading.

He never made reading a chore, always looking for creative ways to get me engaged or bring the content alive. When I was reading about George Washington Carver, he bought peanuts and peanut butter as illustrations of his accomplishments. He also told me that George Washington Carver was successful because he had listened to God. Those words became deeply planted into my heart.

Before the summers' end, I was begging to go to the book-mobile and reading about a book a day. When I was retested right before school started, to determine what grade I would be in, my reading level had jumped to five grades above my class.

We traveled a lot as a family, and Daddy seized every opportunity to make it an adventure of learning. He would point out what was growing in the fields, what type of cows or sheep were grazing in the pastures, and the names of the flowers and the trees we passed. Then he would quiz us afterward and award us with a treat.

On one trip to the Canadian Rockies, Daddy let me have my own hotel room. I was only seven at the time, making his decision a little risky, but he trusted me and must have discerned that I was independent and needed to explore. My room faced Muskoka Lake, and I thought it would be fun to see what would happen if I locked the bathroom door from the outside while the tub was filling. I never thought about how to get back in. When

I realized I was locked out, I ran down the back stairs to the next floor to Mother and Daddy's room, screaming hysterically.

"I told you she was too young," Mother said to Daddy.

Unfazed, he called downstairs to maintenance and reported that the lock on the bathroom door had been pushed in and the tub was running.

A few minutes later, maintenance unlocked the door. The water had just reached the brim and was beginning to pour over the top, so we threw towels down on the floor to mop up the water. I clung to Daddy, certain that I was in deep trouble. From then on, Carmen had the room and I stayed with my parents.

Later that night over dinner, Daddy was recapping the things each of us had learned that day and said with a grin, "Ritalynn learned what happens when you lock the bathroom door from the outside." He didn't shame me or make me feel stupid; he just made it another lesson.

It built my trust in him even more.

———

Daddy involved us in his work and his life, and he would sometimes spontaneously decide to take one of us kids with him on a business trip. By *spontaneous*, I mean that we wouldn't know if one of us was going at all, or who it would be, until we got to the airport.

On one such occasion, we were all gathered at the airport saying goodbye, and just as he was leaving to board the plane, he handed Carmen a ticket and told him that they would buy whatever he needed when they got to their destination. I was so upset that I stormed out of the gate and found a place where I could cry. Mom and Dottie could not find me for hours.

A month later, it was my turn to go with Daddy. This trip was pre-planned just for me; we were going to Washington, DC. Prior to the trip, Daddy escorted me to every type of department store and selected beautiful outfits for me, having me model each one. He even picked out my first set of luggage for the trip. It was pink.

During the day while Daddy was working, I stayed in the hotel. I had books, coloring books and pens, and lots of snacks and drinks. I was by myself, but I never remember feeling alone or scared. Each night after dinner, Daddy and I would sit down at the table and look through AAA travel brochures for different tourist sites in the area. He let me pick out the places I wanted to visit. One day was to be more special than the rest—the day I was to accompany Daddy to one of his important meetings.

I could hardly wait. We picked out my outfit, and at noon sharp, Dad came to the room and escorted me to the car, where some of his business associates waited. I felt so special. He was my hero, my giant. He had explained to me how important this meeting was and that he wanted me to act like a young lady. I was determined to please him.

We were seated at a large center table with eight other dinner guests. The restaurant was beautiful, with white tablecloths, silver, and fine china. The waiter gave me my own menu, but it was so heavy that I had difficulty holding it. I saw shrimp on the menu and assumed it was fried shrimp like we had in Texas. I liked fried shrimp and didn't know that they served it other ways.

The waiter brought out a huge silver dish filled with crushed ice and topped with cold shrimp, complete with their tails sticking up in the air. I guess it was the sophisticated way to eat shrimp, but I did not like cold shrimp. My brother had shown me what live shrimp looked like, with their heads and tails and hundreds of legs, and this looked an awful lot like bait.

I did what only a child would know to do: I pretended to chew and swallow the shrimp while carefully placing each piece of shrimp into my napkin. I could not let Daddy's business associates know that I did not like cold shrimp. "This is so good. Thank you," I said. I had been appropriately trained by the best.

Daddy's business associates remarked what a wonderful young lady I was, and that I had such a healthy appetite for such a petite little girl. Seated across the table from me, Daddy proudly smiled and said, "That's my precious little princess whom I adore."

I just giggled. I was so glad I had made him proud.

The next moment happened so quickly, I didn't see it coming. A tall, overly attentive waiter noticed my cloth napkin all folded up on my lap. He whisked the napkin from my lap and gave it a proper snap in the air to straighten it out so he could place it back the way it belonged. When he did so, all the pieces of shrimp went flying. Women at nearby tables were dodging flying shrimp, some screaming.

I couldn't worry about the other tables; I was fixated on Daddy's horrified face. At that moment, I wanted to dive under the table.

One of Dad's associates seated next to me tried to come to my rescue. "Oh, honey, don't you worry about a thing," he said. "I don't like those cold things either. How would you like a hamburger?"

I was so embarrassed that when my hamburger arrived, I was too ashamed to eat.

Daddy seemed to know what I was feeling. He excused himself, came over to where I was seated, bent over, and whispered, "Ritalynn, you never have to hide something from your daddy. All you had to say was that you didn't like cold shrimp, and I would've gotten you something else." He gave me a big hug and kiss on the cheek. "It's okay, darling. Daddy's not mad. Actually, this place needed to be livened up."

I looked up at him and smiled, and all the embarrassment melted away. He was my hero.

CHAPTER SEVENTEEN

SOMETHING DADDY COULD NOT FIX

DADDY AND MOTHER SEEMED happy in Houston. They continued to attend grand openings and events, and most of the time Carmen and I tagged along. I don't remember exactly when this changed, but a time then came when they started leaving us with babysitters more frequently, and we made it known we didn't like the change.

While playing cowboys and Indians one time, we convinced our babysitter to let us tie her to a chair. We each took the end of a jump rope and ran around in circles until she could not wiggle loose. It started off innocent enough, but once she was bound to the chair, we thought it was fun and left her there while we went into another room to play. The more she protested, the more we laughed and ignored her. She was still knotted to the chair when Mother and Daddy returned home a few hours later. Although we were punished, it resulted in our getting a better babysitter from then on—our grandmother Dee Dee, whom we adored.

Even with Mom and Dad working longer hours and socializing on weekday evenings, they would make as much individual time with each of us as possible. With Carmen, Daddy would dump all the containers of Legos, Lincoln Logs, and Matchbox cars all over the den floor. The two of them would then carefully design and build massive buildings and elaborate roads. They dotted the scenery with cotton balls to resemble snow, and Dad constructed mountains out of a flour-and-water mixture that they'd paint.

They'd also arrange Dad's Lionel train collection around an elaborate home development that Dad designed to look real. It was so painstakingly crafted and beautiful that Mom would allow it to stay up for weeks at a time, and each day we were entertained by the train chugging around the oblong track, puffing smoke from the engine and blowing its whistle.

Mom spent time with me, grooming me to become a little "model" for Christian Women's Club, shopping for beautiful clothes and jewelry, getting manicures, and learning the important social graces that would make me a cultured and refined Southern girl. Being quite the talker, I was often invited to participate on children's television shows to fill in gaps for kids who were too shy. Mom thought this was a perfect opportunity to practice my newly acquired social skills.

I was curious and inquisitive about the nature of God, and some of my favorite times as a family were when Dad would entertain us with spontaneously made-up stories of Hoonda and Boonda, fictionalized characters who traveled on their pet white elephant throughout the African jungles sharing the gospel of Jesus. Dad had a creative and inventive mind, especially when it came to his real passion: sharing about Jesus. As kids, we were mesmerized by Dad's stories.

"Hoonda and Boonda were riding on their big white elephant in the jungles of the African forest. A few days earlier, they had encountered a close meeting with people who did not like them sharing about Jesus and were aggressively trying to stop them. Tanya, their big white pet elephant, had lifted her big trunk into the air and made a resounding bugle sound that alerted all the other elephants. A few minutes later, there was a stampede in the village. Arrows zoomed past Hoonda and Boonda as Tanya's big white hoofs took up speed."

We were all glued, anticipating what came next. I sat straight up in bed, with Carmen and Mom next to me and Dottie and her college friends stretched out on the floor, waiting for Dad to continue.

"Hoonda and Boonda had no idea that the same people from the last village had tracked Tanya's steps. They had uncovered a medicine man who promised he could tranquilize Tanya while the natives captured Hoonda and Boonda from their gondola. This would stop their spreading the story about Jesus.

"'Shhhh. Did you hear that, Boonda?' whispered Hoonda. Tanya's large trunk began to sway way left to far right as if to sense trouble." Daddy imitated the jungle sounds with the inflection of screeches in his voice. "Something was wrong. 'Shhhh. There on the left, Hoonda. I see a reflection over there. Look.' Boonda pointed and spoke just above a whisper. 'Over there, over there.' Tanya began to twitch and became more agitated.

"Over there too, and there. We're surrounded. We're surrounded. We need to pray."

It was like I was living in the story. I felt every emotion and heard every sound in the jungle. "Daddy, Daddy, what happens?" I asked.

"The natives were surrounding the gondola with raised poison-tipped spears aimed toward the children. Hoonda and Boonda stared back at the natives as they clutched each other's hands. Tanya had been given a tranquilizer and was beginning to falter, but ..."

Nightly, no matter who was at our home, at 8 p.m. we all paraded down the hallway to gather in my pink-and-white princess room to find a comfortable spot to listen as Daddy told another story. Many times, people encouraged Daddy to record these stories into a series of children's books, but he never did.

Dad's ingenuity and cleverness was not just with storytelling; it carried over into the way our summer vacations were planned. He always made everything a game. We had "family lottery," where he'd tell Mom, Carmen, Dottie, and me to write down the place we'd most like to go on vacation, anywhere in the continental United States. We folded our papers, put them in a paper bag, and Daddy with his twinkling blue eyes reached inside the bag, stalling and crinkling the paper. Whichever paper he pulled out first was where we went on vacation.

"Hurry, Daddy!" we cried in unison.

"No, I don't think this one is it," he said as he dropped the first folded piece of paper back into the bag. After several minutes of teasing, he'd pull another folded piece of paper from the bag and trumpet, "Da da da daaaaa! Six Flags over Georgia!"

What we did not realize was that Dad had already planned to surprise us with every vacation request in the bag and anything else he thought of along the way. These vacations were weeks long and not only for fun; Dad also used them as another outreach opportunity to share the gospel of Jesus Christ.

He engineered and produced testimonies of famous people of the day and had them professionally printed and rolled in various bright-colored cellophane wrappers that he called "Gospel Bombs." Dad printed our home address and phone number on the tracts so he could answer questions and pray with anyone with a need. The plan was to drive through small towns along the way and toss the cigar-sized tracts out the window while announcing to anyone who might be within earshot, "Gospel Bombs!"

The Gospel Bombs had been a well-received evangelism tool in California. Many people on the West Coast had accepted Christ, contacted my parents for more information, and inquired about a good local church in their area. But this was a different time and place. It was now the early 1960s and we were in the rural Deep South—from Texas through Mississippi, Alabama, and Georgia.

As we drove through my mother's home state of Mississippi, we somehow missed the turn onto the main highway and found ourselves in a rundown section of a small town. In our white 1963 Cadillac, we certainly stood out. Dad never gave it a thought though; he just saw it as an opportunity to share Jesus.

"Kids, it's time for a Gospel Bomb throw. Get ready!" he said.

The two large boxes full of Gospel Bombs were resting in front of my booster seat as I waited for Dad's instructions.

"Now!" Dad shouted.

Windows down, we tossed the colorful cellophane-wrapped testimonies and yelled, "Gospel Bomb!"

As it turned out, nobody heard the word *gospel*, only the word *bomb*. It terrorized the neighborhood. Parents screamed to their children to get into the house, some ducked onto the pavement, and kids cried and ran to the nearest adult. The more they screamed, the louder I screamed, "Gospel Bomb!"

In self-defense, several men and women approached our car, jeering and threatening us while attempting to break Coke bottles against our car windows. They were right beside my window, and it frightened me so much I began to cry hysterically.

"Lionel," Mom said quietly but firmly, "I don't think this was your best idea, do you? We need to get out of here quick."

Daddy said nothing as he quickly navigated us to another part of town. Not a word was spoken for a long time. That was the end of the Gospel Bomb idea.

Upon returning home after one of our several-week-long vacations, Daddy called Carmen and me into the living room. He and Mom had something important to share. "Ritalynn and Carmen, we need you both to know something," he said. "Your daddy is older than your friends' daddies."

I continued playing with my doll.

Daddy repeated his words. There was something in his voice that made me stop playing and look up at him. He was not smiling like he usually was, and the twinkle in his eye was missing.

I dropped my doll, ran to where he was standing, and threw my arms around his legs. "Daddy, I don't care. You're my daddy!" I clung to his legs as he hugged me closer but said nothing more. In my little girl's mind, I could not understand why he would make a special point to tell us this, or why it mattered. But he was my daddy, and I believed he could fix anything.

I don't remember how long after that day—it may have been days or even weeks later—that Carmen and I were swimming in the backyard pool when Mom called me to come in the house.

Daddy had designed the pool and surrounding gardens beautifully, with mature trees, a garage apartment, and tile walkways lined with fragrant gardenias and colorful annuals. This area joined their master bathroom via a sliding glass door, with a cleverly disguised outdoor shower partially enclosed by a privacy wall. Coming out of the pool, we could step directly into the outdoor shower and change into dry clothes in the master bathroom instead of tromping through the main living area in wet bathing suits. But this day, instead of going around through the master bathroom, I followed my mother's voice straight into the living room, wet bathing suit and all.

"Ritalynn, I want to introduce you to Vicki," Mom said. "She's about your age. Will you please take her to your room and get out of that wet bathing suit, dear?"

Daddy had picked out my room, which opened with French doors and had two closets and a beautiful window overlooking our side yard. I had a princess canopy bed with sheer pink lace draping as the canopy overlay, matching dressers, and a dressing table and chair. The room was filled with dolls and books and all the things that would be any child's delight. Daddy called it my "princess room." I loved my room and was always proud to show it off to guests.

With my towel wrapped around me and barefoot, I led Vicki down the hall to my room. I jumped on the bed in my wet clothes, and Vicki said loudly, "Get off my bed!"

I stared at her. "*Your* bed?"

"Yes, this is *my* bed, *my* room."

I had never been spoken to like that before, and I was confused by her saying that my room was hers. Running into the living room where both of our parents were having an intense conversation, I blurted out, "Mommy! Daddy! Vicki said that *my* room and *my* canopy bed is hers!" I was almost crying. "Tell her now it's not true!"

"Ritalynn, we will discuss this later," Mom said.

"No, Mom. You tell her."

But she was silent.

Tears now streamed down my face as I tugged on Daddy's suit jacket. "Daddy, please tell her it's not her room! It's *my* princess room you made just for me!"

Daddy gazed into my eyes, looking like he did not know what to say. He shook his head. "Ritalynn, Vicki and her parents just bought our home and everything in it."

I could not believe it. "But, Daddy, my bed? My canopy bed?"

"Yes, honey. Even your canopy bed."

Vicki stood beside her parents with her arms folded, wearing a smirk on her face. For the first time in my life, I experienced hate. My whole body trembled, my lip quivered, and tears slid down my cheeks.

My whole world had just crumbled, and for the first time, Daddy could not fix it.

Me and my princess bed, Houston

CHAPTER EIGHTEEN

Lost Money, Lost Gospel, Lost Joy

I COULD HARDLY COMPREHEND THE overwhelming sense of loss I felt as, piece by piece, our life as we knew it fell apart. One by one, people came to the door and took each of our family pets—my rabbits and parakeets—to a new home. They could not go with us to our new house. The only pet we could keep was Ginger, our two-year-old German Shepherd.

I choked back tears as I stuffed my last doll into a suitcase and looked around my princess room for the last time. I could still see the look on Vicki's face, and I could not think of her living in my room and sleeping in my canopy bed. Tanglewood had no apartments near it, so we moved into a small two-bedroom, one-bath apartment in the Barcelona Apartments across town, literally on the other side of the tracks. It was a far cry from our large, sprawling home with a pool. Anything that did not fit in our flat was left behind.

Almost everything about the way we lived our life changed. Mom began working longer hours with Dad to bring in extra money, so Carmen and I were placed in a rudimentary after-school care program affiliated with the church. No more private nannies, no more daily trips to the toy store, no fun and games for hours in our backyard pool. Now we were allowed only a brief time outside to play hopscotch or jump rope, followed by a nap on old army cots and snacks of store-bought graham crackers and juice. We were usually trapped there until after sunset.

The one exception was when my Brownie troop would get together. I loved being a part of a local troop, exploring new things, earning badges for community service and good acts at home, and selling cookies. On the days when the Brownies met, Carmen would tag along just to get away from the church daycare. Neither of us particularly liked it. I wanted to have my own space, and he was embarrassed being the only boy. The only saving grace was that the moms took turns bringing homemade desserts and Coca-Colas.

Our apartment was small and cramped, and Daddy recognized that we needed other outlets for play. Not only that, I needed activities apart from my brother. Daddy discovered slot-car racing, a competitive hobby of racing powered miniature autos guided on grooved tracks. There was a huge public track near our apartment.

Since it was traditionally a hobby for boys, Carmen competed first and I just watched. I quickly got bored and soon convinced Daddy to let me try my hand at controlling the car. At seven years old, I was the only girl racer at the track. I learned quickly, and soon I could beat my brother and every other boy.

I could also take my car apart and put it back together in record time. Every Saturday, I packed my little briefcase full of racing miniatures, extra tires, oil, petite pliers, wires, and anything else that might repair a wrecked-up car. I loved going fast and was soon bringing home ribbons every weekend. Winning seemed to temporarily fill the hole left in my heart.

Sure, I missed our lifestyle, but most of all, I missed my daddy. He just wasn't the same. He seemed preoccupied and moody, and became rigid and often gruff. And he worked on Sundays now. He wasn't the daddy I knew.

One day, he announced that we were all going to St. Petersburg, Florida, for several weeks. He had identified potential investors and partners who were interested in buying the Serrano Hotel and transforming it into a retirement community like the one he successfully developed in Santa Barbara, The Samarkand. Carmen and I were taken out school, and Mom brought along our school assignments so we kept up with our studies.

Once in Florida, I quickly became bored with the daily routine. No matter who showered first, I was dressed ahead of everyone else and did my best to boss them to finish more quickly. "Carmen, put on these shorts. Daddy, wear this shirt. Mom, you don't need makeup." I had one speed—full throttle—and I was ready to start the day.

Because of my persistence, Mom and Daddy gave me permission to go downstairs to the café and eat breakfast ahead of them. I attracted plenty of attention when I walked into the café by myself. What I did not know was that Dad had already called the manager and they were expecting my arrival. I sat on the red plastic swivel chair at the counter and placed my order:

one link of sausage, buttered rye toast, and a small fresh orange juice. With my 77 cents in my purse, I felt all grown up.

Tackling breakfast by myself was just the first step. Soon after lunch, while Carmen was taking his usual afternoon nap and Mother and Daddy were working, I set out to explore the hotel on my own. In the lobby, I discovered a group that was rehearsing a Hawaiian-themed play to be performed four days later.

As I watched and clapped, a man approached me. "Hello, my name is Sam. We would all like to know if you would join our play."

"Yes, yes!" I squealed with delight. I had met new friends and I was going to sing and dance, and wear a hula skirt, a pretty bikini top, and flip flops.

Excitedly, I raced to tell Mother and Daddy all about it. He didn't respond, and she didn't seem to share my excitement. I chalked their reaction up to their being absorbed in their work. Then the night of the performance came, and I had reserved front-row seats for my family. I was excited for them to watch me perform and threw my arms around everyone for a goodbye kiss.

"Ritalynn," Daddy said, stiffening, "we are not coming. It's disgraceful that you would be involved in show business. It's worldly. I will not let your mother or brother come."

I was devastated. What had I done wrong? Why was Daddy upset with me? I burst from the room crying and ran down the hall to the elevator. No one came after me. Surely he didn't mean that, and they would come watch my play. But as I joined the other kids and danced and sang my heart out, I peered through the crowd of onlookers searching for Daddy, Mom, and Carmen. They were not there.

When our cast party was over, I skipped the elevator and ran up the twelve flights of stairs to our penthouse floor. I pounded on the door. Daddy quietly opened it, turned around, and returned to reading his Bible, saying nothing. Carmen and Mom continued reading books. No one congratulated me or asked me how I did. In fact, no one paid attention to me at all.

Things returned to normal by the next day, but once again, I became bored with sitting around the hotel. I remembered my best friend, Anne, who had lived next door to us a few years before when we lived in St. Petersburg, and asked Mom to call her house. Anne invited me to go with her family to see the movie *Mary Poppins*.

I was excited to go, so I ran down to the hotel lobby where Daddy was talking to some people and barged right in. "Daddy, Anne wants me to go with her to see *Mary Poppins*!"

He excused himself and took me aside. "Darling," he said quietly, "we don't go to movies. They're not good, they're bad."

Once again, I did not understand such a strong reaction over what seemed like an innocent thing. This was so unlike Daddy. He was different. Later, Mom convinced him to let me go with Anne, but throughout the entire movie, all I could think about was that Daddy did not want me there.

He must have been thinking about his reaction too. The next day he invited me to go for a walk on the beach with him.

I grabbed my swim suit, running full tilt with one foot in one leg hole while trying to pull my shorts over the suit.

"Ritalynn, Daddy is not leaving you," he said. "You're all tangled up. Let me help you. I know that I've been a little gruff and I'm sorry. I'm trying to give you everything you need and want."

I looked up at him and smiled. "Daddy, I need Anne to be in our family. Will you call her daddy and tell him that you want to adopt her, for *me*?" I was lonely and needed another built-in playmate.

Outside, he took me into a phone booth and dialed the rotary phone. "Richard, this is Lionel Mayell. You know we love Anne and your family." He went on to promise that he would love Anne and treat her as his own.

I could have sworn Daddy had called. But Anne never came to be my sister.

When we returned to our apartment in Houston, we started attending a different church. I had loved going to Second Baptist Church, but now we were at Long Point Baptist, a smaller, very Southern Baptist-style church. The people in the church yelled and, from my perspective, seemed forced to go down to the altar after singing the same song several times. Daddy became more rigid and on edge, and every time the doors opened in the church, we had to be there. It was no longer fun because it had become more of a demand to attend than a choice.

The services were long and boring, and I did not like sitting. The only thing that was amusing was this one lady who walked the aisle every Sunday, crying as she pulled her wedding ring off her left hand and dropped it in the offering plate in front of everyone.

"Mommy, how many rings does she have?" I asked loudly.

Embarrassed, Mom quickly shushed me.

It was like magic. The next week the woman had another ring to place in the bucket.

The longer we went to this church, the stricter and less joyful Daddy became. We could not play on Sundays because it was the Lord's Day. We could not watch television on Sunday, nor could I sit with my friends in the back of the church. I had to sit up front with my family and behave like a lady. I always loved it when Mom had an excuse not to go on Sunday nights, like when Daddy needed to go to the office. As soon as Daddy pulled away from the apartment, Mom let us turn the TV on to watch *Bonanza*. It was our secret. I never understood why it was okay for Daddy to work on Sundays, but not for me to watch television.

One of my friends from school invited me to go with her and her mother to the Texas rodeo. She was the first friend I had whose parents were not living together. Daddy did not want me to go because her mother was divorced. I did not understand; my friend had nothing to do with what her parents chose.

Reluctantly, Daddy agreed I could go. "Ritalynn, here is five dollars to spend. Now don't be foolish with this. It's hard to come by these days."

I took the money as if it were a million dollars and folded it up in my coin purse that fit perfectly in my purse.

The *Bonanza* television family was there. I loved Little Joe (Michael Landon) on the series, but thought Daddy might disapprove, so instead I bought an autographed picture of his big brother Hoss with my $5. When I got home, the first thing I did was run to where Daddy was, proud to show him my picture. "Daddy, look what I bought!"

Daddy took one look at the picture. "How could you be so foolish, Ritalynn? Is this how I taught you?" His tone was harsh, his words harsher.

I felt so shamed by him. I ripped my picture of Hoss into tiny pieces and ran to my room, slamming the door as I threw myself across the bed in tears. At the time, I thought life couldn't get worse, but I was wrong.

When we had been living in the apartment for over a year, Daddy called a family meeting. Dottie could not attend because she was living in London at the time, working with the Billy Graham Crusade, so Carmen and I joined Mom and Dad.

"Children," he began solemnly, "our business, Mayell Enterprises, and all of its subsidiaries are closing. Circumstances beyond our control have happened. People we believed were on our team made some unwise decisions, and unfortunately it has created a financial burden for our family. But your mother and I trust God over man, and we believe God is using this to gain our attention. He has given us three opportunities to choose. I want you children to have a vote in where we go. The first choice is to work with Billy Graham and move to Montreat, North Carolina. The second is to move to California and be a part of Campus Crusade for Christ. Or my friend Walt Disney, the founder of Disneyland, has asked if I would be the developer of condominiums in a new concept in Florida he is calling Disney World. He has a home for us including a dock and boat and college tuition paid for you kids, and we will be back living in Florida."

I had no idea what the impact of any decision would be. All I heard was California, and I liked the mountains. When we took a vote, it was a tie. Carmen and Mom chose North Carolina, and Daddy and I chose California. None of us chose Florida.

That summer, Bill and Vonette Bright invited our family to spend a month in Cuernavaca, Mexico, in the Chula Vista Hotel, the new Latin American headquarters for Campus Crusade. It would give us an opportunity to meet some of the staff and learn from experience if joining the staff was the right thing for our family. One of Dad's former Christian business friends and his wife were also there, so Mom and Daddy seemed excited.

Living in Cuernavaca, I became fast friends with a few of the Crusade staff children, including Bill Bright's two sons. We had fun roaming and investigating the halls of the large beautiful Chula Vista Hotel. Gorgeous Spanish architecture and a basement with secret doors and back-entrance staircases were a curious child's dream to explore. The hotel property had two beautiful swimming pools, one with a slide surrounded by gardens.

One of my new girlfriends dared me to go down the slide and into the pool. I was wearing a brand-new pair of patent leather shoes that Mom and Daddy had splurged and bought for me just for our trip to Mexico. Excited to take her up on the dare, I took off my new shoes and bathing suit cover-up and went squealing down the slide into the cold water.

When we were ready to leave, I could not find my shoes. I panicked and began to cry as I searched the surrounding area. I found one shoe in a nearby bush and, hours later, the other shoe lying by the kitchen door, completely ripped apart by a dog. In my eight-year-old mind, I must have reacted to the financial pressure my parents were feeling.

By July, our family of five was back in Houston and jam-packed in our white 1965 Cadillac. Mom and Dad were in the front seat, and Dottie and Carmen sat on either side of me in the back-seat. Earlier that day, we had said goodbye to our four-year-old German Shepherd, Ginger, as my brother's good friend Gary came to take her to live with him on his family's ranch. Daddy had said we could not take Ginger because we did not know where we would be living, and it would be unfair to her. Both Mom and Daddy repeatedly promised, "When we get to California, we will get another dog or any pet you desire."

At that moment, promises seemed empty to me. I had experienced so much loss. I had already given up my parakeets and my rabbits, and now I was leaving Ginger, my best friend. As the Houston skyline became distant, I leaned my head back, biting my lip and trying not to cry. Dottie openly sobbed and Carmen scowled, his face red from tears and his head pressed against the window.

Occasionally I would catch Mom or Daddy dabbing their eyes, and Dad would squeeze Mom's hand as if to say it would be okay. But at that moment, nothing about my life was okay.

Ever the optimist, Mom tried to cheer us up with games. "Let's all play the game of finding things outside the car that begin with the letters of the alphabet."

This time it did not work. She tried another game, but the only response was silence.

Daddy tried. "Kids, we're on an adventure! The beautiful snowcapped mountains, sandy beaches, Disneyland, swimming pools." He began to paint word pictures of our new life, and in no time, we all settled in for the long drive to Southern California, dreaming about the new things to come.

CHAPTER NINETEEN

ONLY GOD

FIFTEEN HUNDRED MILES AND two long days later, we pulled into the entrance to Arrowhead Springs Hotel, seven miles north of San Bernardino. I had been sound asleep on my sister's shoulder, but I woke up when the car slowed down, then craned my neck to see where we were.

"We're here," Mom announced softly as she lowered her window and pulled up to the manned security gate that guarded the 1,900-acre headquarters of Campus Crusade for Christ. The brisk California mountain air sent a chill down my spine, and I snuggled with my sister to stay warm while gazing all around to ensure I would not miss anything.

After Mom's brief exchange with the guard, he pressed a button to the automatic gate that granted us entrance to a dark, winding two-lane road. I leaned over Carmen, noticing dimly lit palm trees in the middle of the road mixed with pink and white flowered shrubs. Dad called them oleanders. With each twist of the road, our headlights revealed hints of the surrounding landscape: beautiful cactus and scrub bushes covering the rugged mountains on our left and a deep gorge on the right. Mom hugged the right side of the road as an oncoming car passed us going toward the guard gate. I squeezed Dottie's hand. There was nothing to stop us from going over the edge.

Now fully awake, I peppered Dad with questions until I got the full history of Arrowhead Springs and how it got its name.

Years before, the Serrano Indians in the area followed a large geologic formation on the side of the mountain that they believed pointed to the artesian hot springs in the canyon below. The hot springs were believed to bring physical and spiritual healing, and became the centerpiece for the Serrano, other Indian tribes, and many Spanish missionaries as well.

In the mid-1860s, a tuberculosis and healing sanitarium was built and a type of water-cure branch of medicine called hydropathy was practiced. The sanitarium facility included a steam cave and mud baths, and was later expanded into a hotel, which drew an increasing number of visitors as tourism and settlement in Southern California blossomed. That hotel burned down in a wildfire, and a second hotel was built in 1880s, but ten years later, it too was destroyed in a fire. A third hotel was built in 1905 and promoted "the hottest springs in the world," with temperatures of 196 degrees.

During the 1930s and 1940s, the Arrowhead Resort attracted many visitors from the Hollywood royalty. Humphrey Bogart and Esther Williams even filmed movie scenes there. Unfortunately, another fire burned the resort down again. Rebuilt soon thereafter, the Arrowhead Resort property was commissioned as a naval hospital during World War II and was later purchased by Conrad Hilton.

The resort flourished again for a while, but ultimately its popularity languished as the wealthy and famous gained access to international resort destinations thanks to air travel. Like many other resorts in inland Southern California, the Arrowhead Springs Resort passed into near-anonymity until Campus Crusade for Christ purchased the property in 1962. Dad always said, "God kept it for Crusade."

When we rounded the final bend, there stood a stunning six-story white hotel with graceful columns. Landscaped with fountains, beautiful flowers, palm trees, and a row of flags representing the many countries in which Crusade had offices, it looked more like an oasis in the desert. This grand palace—the place where Elizabeth Taylor and Nicky Hilton once honeymooned, where Esther Williams swam laps and many celebrities frequented—was now my new home.

At that moment and as if perfectly rehearsed, several hundred college students appeared from every direction as chimes from a nearby chapel began to bong twelve times. It was midnight.

Mom paralleled parked, squealing, "Look! See how sharp these kids are? This is why we're here! You can just tell they love Jesus, with their Bibles clutched to their chests and smiles on their faces!"

Daddy wiped tears of joy from his eyes as he jumped out of the passenger's seat and opened Mom's door. "We will probably be a little while. Dottie, why don't you take your brother and sister back down the hill to San Bernardino and see if you can find something to eat."

Dottie had previously visited Arrowhead Springs and knew of a twenty-four-hour taco stand, so off we went.

"What's a taco?" Carmen and I asked.

"Oh, you both are going to love it! It has ground beef, cheese, tomatoes, and sauce, all packed into a crispy shell. Don't worry, your sis will show you how to eat one."

At the taco stand, Dottie, wearing her favorite multicolored flowered dress, carefully tried to unwrap several tacos and juggle assorted sauces and drinks on her lap. As she tore open a packet of hot sauce with her teeth, it squirted all over her dress. She grabbed a napkin and dipped it into the water, then dabbed her dress as she cried, "Oh, Jesus, please don't let this stain!"

Neither Carmen nor I could console her. The napkin was shredded from multiple attempts to remove the sauce, but even with dry cleaning, the stain on her dress could not be removed.

It would be years later before I understood my sister's overreaction to the hot-sauce incident. What I did not know at the time was that she had been forced to drop out of Wheaton College because my parents could no longer afford it. She must have been feeling the strain of the financial pressure, just like I had when my shoes were destroyed by the dog earlier that summer in Mexico.

Around 1 a.m., our family and a front desk attendant with a loaded luggage cart crowded into the oldest elevator I had ever seen. Everyone was quiet but me. I was curious about this beautiful elevator with a gilded brass outer cage that operated manually. The attendant, Amy, a college student working and attending Crusade's summer Bible institute, sat down on a small stool and pushed a brass knob for the sixth floor. I fired questions at her until Mom said, "Ritalynn darling, I know you're excited and curious, but I'm sure Amy is tired."

I had not noticed that Mom and Daddy were drained. Mom was forty-eight and Daddy, sixty-nine. They had just closed their business, moved away from all their friends, and had no idea what God had in store for their lives. They resolutely stood on the belief that this was where God had led. And if He led them, it had to be good.

For the next several weeks, we lived in the three-room suite where Nicky Hilton and Elizabeth Taylor honeymooned. Often, we would get calls from the front desk asking if a visitor could see where the famous couple honeymooned. That meant we had to keep our rooms spotless and ready to show at all times. Both Mom and Dad talked about our living in the hotel as if it were a vacation rather than to admit the reality: we had no money for a home, or even groceries. Our meals were included, so the only thing we needed were our clothes and toiletries.

These were the early years of Campus Crusade ministry. The staff was small. The groundbreaking evangelism tool known as the Four Spiritual Laws had just been written by founder Bill Bright. Josh McDowell was just starting to write and speak, and Hal Lindsey had just completed his first book, *The Late Great Planet Earth*. Andre Kole had recently launched his illusionist ministry. The Military Ministry had just begun, and the first beach outreach for college students provided hands-on evangelism training in preparation for sharing the gospel back on their college campuses.

Campus Crusade grew rapidly during this time, and it continued to explode over the next decade, riding the crest of the wave of the Jesus Movement in California in the late 1960s and early 1970s, including Explo '72 held in the Cotton Bowl, where close to one hundred thousand young people met to be trained and empowered to take the gospel to their campuses. Arrowhead Springs was the place to be, and I was in the middle of it all.

That first week in California, I was enrolled in a day camp with other staff kids my age from all over the United States. My girlfriend who I had played with all summer in Mexico lived in one of the surrounding bungalows next to the hotel, as did some of the guy friends I had made.

My parents were entrenched in the Institute of Biblical Studies, the foundational requirement for all staff members. This was an intense course, extending over several weeks and requiring them to take exams and learn how to share their testimony publicly, how to witness using the Four Spiritual Laws, and how to disciple others. Mom and Dad sat in all-day classes that stretched into late-evening classes. Every time I saw my parents, they were studying and quizzing each other.

While Dottie and Carmen attended classes with Mom and Dad, I was free to have fun with the other staff kids. For the first time, I had friends my age where I lived. We all loved Jesus, and we had very few limits and no curfew. We played Kick the Can, climbed on hotel balconies, played pranks on hotel guests, and swam in the famed Olympic-sized pool until our eyes burned from the chlorine. It was a summer paradise.

There were other differences too. Dinnertime was no longer a small, private family affair, but was held in a large dining hall and shared with hundreds of summer-staff kids in their late teens and early twenties, all of whom were strangers to me. Night after night, Daddy told stories while mother chimed in, and soon our table became the place to eat. It was common for the college age kids to rush through their meal and pull up a chair to hear another of Dad's stories about God's faithfulness in taking someone with ordinary talents and making him extraordinary—all because he found Jesus.

Often, our family closed down the dining room, with Mom and Dad surrounded by kids asking endless questions late into the evening: "How did you end up on staff? Has it been difficult for you to raise your support? What did you do before coming here?"

I had some of the same questions. How *did* we end up here? Our life had certainly changed, and not all for the better, in my opinion. I had lost my princess bed, said goodbye to my pets and my dog Ginger, and moved to a strange place. Mom filled in as the elevator operator and washed the hotel shower curtains by hand alongside Mrs. Bright.

Dad explained, "God does not share His glory with anyone, so He took my money."

I was only eight years old, but I had questions, like would Jesus really take Dad's money. Unlike Dottie and Carmen, I was not afraid to speak up, and my parents were quick to point that out. I questioned why my new friends could play on Sunday but I could not. I questioned why my new friends could go to movies and dances and play cards but I could not. My friends loved Jesus too, and so did their moms and dads. Up until that time, all my friends had believed and behaved the same way I did, so this was the first time I was confronted with people who believed differently. Who was right? By the end of that summer, I had plenty of questions but no good answers.

I noticed that Mom and Dad were a lot older than my friends' parents too. Most of my friends' parents on full-time Crusade staff were half their age. While Mom and Dad never gave their age a second thought, it bothered me, and I began to feel like I was different and that I didn't fit in with the other kids or even my family.

In the fall, I was enrolled in public school for the first time, starting in fourth grade. For a while, I rode the bus with all my friends from Arrowhead Springs down the mountain to San Bernardino. I looked forward to riding a school bus with my new friends, thinking it would be a continuation of the innocent fun and games we'd enjoyed all summer, but nothing could have been further from the truth.

I encountered coarse language and risqué behavior that I had never been exposed to before, and, even worse, the staff kids joined in. This only intensified my feelings of being an outsider, as I was mocked and shamed for not participating. I did not know how to tell my parents. They believed everything was perfect, and I could not be the one to tell them differently.

Evenings as a family in our tiny hotel room only added to the tension. The summer-staff kids were gone, so the dining room was mostly empty and the hours my parents spent mentoring and encouraging teens were a thing of the past. Now Mom and Dad were faced with the reality of raising their own support, and they spent hour after hour making personal calls and writing letters to friends and people they had helped in the past, asking them for financial support. I had never heard my parents even discuss money before, much less deal with not having enough.

"Lionel, no one believes that we don't have any money," I overheard Mom say. "We don't have wealthy parents to support us like these young kids do. What are we going to *do*?"

"Sweetheart, God has never failed us yet and will not now," Dad reassured her. "I don't know what we are going to do, but the burden to figure it out is not upon us, but on Him. God will provide. He loves us. We just simply need to believe. Besides, we're all together as a family."

That conversation would become an all-too-familiar one over the next decade. It would take the next seven years for my parents to raise barely half of their support. Seven years of below-poverty-level income for a family of five. No one could have foreseen how different, and how difficult, our lives would become, but it was the very situation God used to develop a deep, abiding trust that forever changed the way my parents lived.

Soon, we had to move out of the hotel at Arrowhead Springs, and the only way we could buy a house was to borrow the money my sister received as settlement from a car accident for the down payment. Going to church became all about support-raising and not about worship or Sunday School for Carmen and me. My parents identified two churches where we knew people who might be interested in supporting our family, each one about sixty-five miles from our new home in San Bernardino, but in opposite directions.

On Sundays, Mom and Dad dressed us up to make the 130-mile round trip to Lake Avenue Congregational Church in Pasadena, where we dutifully sat on display as Mom and Dad shared their newly written testimony of how they were led by God to join the staff of Campus Crusade for Christ. On Wednesdays, we drove 120 miles round trip in the opposite direction to Palm Springs Community Church and repeated the performance.

No matter what my parents did, no matter who we went to lunch with after church, the money did not come in. One of the churches refused to allow Dad to speak in the main sanctuary because he had been divorced. Faithfully, Dad spent every evening on the phone trying to convince people to support us. I remember him coming home with their paycheck—zero dollars. Campus Crusade had no retirement fund or health benefits in the early years, although there was a doctor onsite at headquarters if we needed one.

To me, support-raising didn't feel like a faith exercise; it felt like begging, and I was getting tired of the performance. In Texas, because we lived an affluent lifestyle of jet-setting, private swimming pools, and lavish vacations, I never felt I was missing out on anything. Now money was always an issue, and at times I felt afraid and even resentful of how our lives had changed. We sold all our nice furniture, Oriental rugs, and expensive antiques. We gave our organ and piano to Campus Crusade. We had one car that sometimes worked and sometimes didn't. Mom now cleaned her own house, and because Dad was concerned about her ruining her hands, I took on the responsibility of helping out.

Financially, we lived moment to moment. While I was convinced this was all a mistake, Dad was certain it was an opportunity not only to believe but also to *expect* God to do new and big things for our family. He began to shift our focus away from raising support and toward anticipation and expectation. And that's when the miracles started to happen.

"Kids," Dad said one evening as we gathered around the table, "we have a wonderful Savior, and He is our sole provider. We have no money for this month, but God will provide. I want us as a family to come together and pray, because I believe God will show up. First, let us praise Him not for the situation, but because He is God."

The answers to prayers weren't always immediate, but they formed an unmistakable pattern of the hand of God. The doorbell would ring and there would be bags of groceries left on our front porch by an anonymous giver. The phone would ring, and the bank manager would tell Dad that someone had put a thousand dollars in our account. Our car would break down, and when Dad went to pick it up from the garage, the bill had already been paid.

Another time, someone from Texas called and said they were driving their two-year-old Oldsmobile to California because God told them we needed a car. Still another time, a dealer in Los Angeles called and told us that a new car had been paid for in our name. When entering a grocery store, Mom set off a bell because she was the one-hundredth customer, and the manager gave her a much needed $100 gift certificate to buy food for our family.

Mom was a wonderful cook, and she and Daddy loved to invite people over for a meal just to love them and encourage them in their faith. Our electric stove wasn't particularly reliable though, and once, in the middle of meal preparation for seventeen people, the electric burners would not heat. As my ten-year-old self watched from around a corner, Mom prayed over the stove, "Father, we don't have any money for this meal, and now the stove doesn't work. You are powerful, and you placed it in our hearts to love these guests. So you make the stove work."

She fiddled with the coils and the electrical wiring, but the burner would not heat. Again she prayed and asked God to make the stove work. The third time, the burners turned red and never quit again the entire night. When the handyman came to check it out the next day, he was confused because the electrical system was burned out and should have never turned on. She shared what God did, then prayed for him and his family.

Although miracles happened frequently, there were also many times when the phone never rang and the answers didn't come, at least not immediately. My parents prayed and cried, but pushed through their tears to hold on to God. Life was not always easy, and many times my parents went without so we kids wouldn't have to.

One of those times, I wanted a new dress. I was a young teen and was struggling with my self-image. Daddy took me shopping and picked out a new dress and shoes for me. It wasn't until we arrived back home that I noticed the cardboard inserts he had placed in his shoes to cover the holes in his soles.

Another time, Mom kept making excuses not to sit down and enjoy dinner with the rest of us. She was either "not hungry" or "just too busy." I realized later that she did not join us because there was not enough food to go around. At times she stretched out the meat with rice and oats and noodles to make it last two meals. Other times I saw Daddy pick citrus fruit from our trees and have that by itself for his evening meal, explaining that he was still satisfied from lunch and didn't want a full meal.

As God's miraculous provision became part of the pattern of our family life, the concerns I once had about my parents being "different" became less important, and were replaced by the excitement of anticipating what God would do next. Even when no miracles came and we had no money, I knew in my spirit that God would provide.

I still wrestled with the question of how we ended up here—going from a life of privilege and plenty to "begging" for monetary support. I wanted to know the real answer. I'm sure I heard these words many times as a child and as a teenager, but it wasn't until I read my parents' written testimonies as an adult that I began to truly understand their process and their struggles.

In an excerpt from Dad's testimony, he explained how he believed God had been calling him for years into full-time ministry, and how even though he had other opportunities after he lost his business, he felt that on Crusade staff was where they were to be:

> For many years, the Lord had called me to serve Him in a more dynamic way. But the more money I made, the more I wanted to make. My developments at first were modest in size, and then they grew into gigantic, multimillion-dollar enterprises. One company grew into many corporations, spreading from several California corporations across the country to the East Coast, into Florida and Texas. THE LORD CONTINUALLY CALLED ME TO GET OUT OF BUSINESS, and I found myself saying, "The only way I will ever answer God's call is for God to whip me down, and not until then will I ever give up to Him." I was frightened at my own introspection.
>
> Then one year came when the Lord allowed me to see everything slip away. Every bit of property, every homeplace, everything—even borrowing to the limit from time to time on our insurance. Strange as it may seem to you, I was not frustrated. I did not commit suicide. Nor did my sweet wife divorce me. Somehow, in all of these tragic episodes, we felt that our wonderful Lord had permitted it all for a purpose, for a reason all His own.
>
> We just knew that He had a great plan for our lives. And this plan we knew He had conceived before the

foundations of the world. Terrific! What a great God! What would His plan be? We continually prayed for His will to be revealed.

I only knew one business. I had organized, constructed, and sold developments totaling upwards of $100 million. I then created master designs for several new projects. They did not enthuse me, but this is all I could do. ... The president of a big finance company in Houston gave me an oral commitment for financing. I was not interested, although I kept moving and kept praying.

In a miraculous way, our wonderful friend Dr. Bill Bright ... invited Dorothy and myself to Arrowhead Springs to consider coming on staff and using our construction experience in that great work. To join the Campus Crusade staff was farthest from our minds, but when we were invited we both said, "THIS IS IT!"

Mom's testimony provides additional insights into their emotional journey and the difficulty of raising support:

We discovered that God didn't want our money, our possessions, position—He wanted us, just us. We saw that we could be a success in man's eyes and yet a failure in God's. God gives, and God takes away. ... He took, or allowed us to lose, all of our money, all of our homes, including all of the furnishings, insurance, savings, our business, our cars except for one, and a very few family antiques and organ. I guess the Lord knew we had to come to Him empty-handed as far as "things" were concerned. I don't know what we would have done if we had not known the reality of Jesus Christ and had the power to live the abundant life. We didn't even hate the man who was supposed to be a Christian, who double-crossed us and caused all this. We felt sorry for him and prayed for him. Only Christ will give you the power to do that.

We prayed and asked the Lord what He wanted us to do with our lives. I told the Lord we were too old to be missionaries, and I especially couldn't be one in Mexico because every time I went there, I would get very ill. ... We had known Dr. and Mrs. Bright before Campus Crusade was in existence. Lionel kept saying, "Let us drive out to CCC and see what is going on." We had to have some money to pay some bills and for expenses on the trip, so we prayed. We never asked any of our friends for a loan—because we had always been on the giving end, and we still had some pride.

You will never guess how He helped us out. One day in the mail was a letter from the IRS. ... The first thing I thought was, *Oh no, a mistake has been made by the auditors, and we will have to pay more taxes.* How I prayed before I opened that letter! Well, it was a letter telling us that two years ago we had overpaid the government, and enclosed was a check for $12,000. On the letter, they mentioned that the check was to have been sent a year ago, and they couldn't understand what had happened. Well, I did. The Lord knew when we were going to need it most. It paid the bills, and we left for Campus Crusade.

Now came the real testing time. I had known about supporting CCC people because we had helped many of them. I didn't think the time would ever come when we would have to lower ourselves in asking friends to support us. ... I said to Lionel, "You know how well they [Dr. and Mrs. Bright] know us, and how we have supported CCC since it began. We have never asked anyone for anything before. They won't ask us to do that!" We weren't there ten minutes before Bill Bright made us feel as though raising support was a privilege.

The next two and a half years were a real testing time for each of us. ... We did not return to our beautiful home in Altadena because it was gone, but we found a place in San Bernardino—a place we always said we would never live. We sent out two hundred support letters, and many of these people had become wealthy because of my husband. You know, we did not receive half our support for years. We sold our organ and some personal things. You would not believe the strange excuses some of the people would write for not sending any money. One day, after reading some letters, my carnal nature began to show and then the next day, a former maid of ours sent something. I cried when I received that. ... Many a time, it was difficult for me to say thank you.

Lionel had many fantastic offers to go back into business, but we both agreed that this was where the Lord wants us. He would show us if He didn't want us here anymore, but we had no desire to do anything differently.

———

People continue to question how my parents lost their money. I really don't know. My brother and sister have varying accounts. What I do know is that someone double-crossed us, as Mom said, and that caused us to lose our money. In fact, what I know based on Mom's testimony is that our money was drained from our bank account. Back in those days, our family bank account was joined with the Mayell business account. Was it an employee or financial investor? I will never know. But not knowing is evidence that neither of my parents ever spoke ill will against anyone. All I remember is that we prayed for this person without using their name. The biggest lesson in this story is not losing our money, but how my parents navigated through this painful and difficult transition. It was never without struggle, but they learned firsthand God's faithfulness. They grew in their trust, deepened in their faith, and learned to rest in His love.

Mom and Dad on staff with Campus Crusade, 1977

No Fear

WHILE BEING ON STAFF with Campus Crusade for Christ brought tremendous financial challenges, relying on God for our basic needs built Dad's faith that much stronger. It also released in him a new freedom and a boldness to share his faith. Maybe it was because he had personally experienced how fickle wealth and popularity can be, and because he knew firsthand what it was like to experience deep rejection. Dad became singularly focused on a person's need to know Christ, no matter who they were and no matter what their social status. He had always been bold, but he developed a fearlessness in sharing his faith that became the very trait to reach the unreachable.

―――――

"Jesus, Jesus, Jesus," Mom whispered as if to assure herself.

I had been asleep for most of the seventy-mile trip from Palm Springs back to our home in San Bernardino, but being a light sleeper, I awakened when I heard something unfamiliar in my mother's voice.

"What's wrong, Mom?" I asked.

"Nothing for you to worry about, darling. Go back to sleep."

"Come on. What's going on?" I spoke loudly enough to awaken Dad in the passenger seat. One by one, all three of our sleepy heads popped up.

"Darling, is something the matter?" he inquired.

"A car's been following us," she said. "What do I do?"

"For how long, Dorothy?"

"I noticed it when we got on Interstate 10, about ten minutes into our drive."

"Can you see who the driver is?"

"It's a man, but I can't see much with the bright headlights. Now that you're all awake, he's staying farther back. I don't like this, Lionel."

"Don't go to the house," Daddy instructed. "Keep driving."

In the silence that followed, I knew Daddy was praying. Not even a minute later, his voice was calm and assured. "Mother, go ahead home now. It'll be okay. Besides, Carmen left his baseball bat in the trunk from Saturday's game."

"But if we drive into the driveway, we can be blocked in," she pointed out. "We don't have an automatic garage door."

"Mother, I believe we will be fine. How do you know that this isn't an opportunity to share Christ with someone?"

"Oh, Lionel, for once ..." She sighed. "I still don't like this."

Before Mom could bring the car to a complete stop, Dad had pushed the trunk release in the glove box, grabbed the bat, and was striding toward the man's car. "Why are you following us?"

he demanded. He stood erect, shoulders wide, doing his best to look menacing.

None of us could hear the man's answer. As the car door slowly opened, I held my breath. A large, athletic-built man with dark skin stepped out. Daddy was almost half his size and weight. This man looked as if he could snap Carmen's bat in half like a pencil, but Daddy stood eye to eye with him, engaged in a brief exchange.

The man told Dad that he was unfamiliar with the area and had taken a wrong turn and gotten lost, but then he saw our Texas license plate. He needed to get to Houston to see his mother who was dying, and had recognized our Harris County tags. He thought by following us he might be led in the right direction.

Dad believed the man was telling the truth. "What's your name?"

"Henry Trottman, sir."

"Well, Henry, have you eaten? It is a long drive to Houston and you must eat."

"No sir, I have not."

Dad looked at us. "Mother darling, will you go into the house and fix Henry something to eat? He's hungry."

Mom hesitated. I could tell she was not keen on Dad's request to invite a total stranger inside. He could overpower all of us if he had wanted.

Dad pulled gently on Henry's long-sleeved blue dress shirt, ushering him through the front door. After pointing to the most comfortable chair in the living room for Henry to sit, he went into his office and pulled out his AAA maps that were already marked from our drive from Houston to San Bernardino.

He spread the maps out on the dining room table, then began to outline in a different color marker the route that Henry would need to follow to get to his mother's home in Houston. As he was drawing the route, he casually called out, "Hey, Henry, do you know Jesus?"

"No, but my mother's been praying," came the response from the living room.

"Didn't you say she doesn't have long to live? I bet it would be a real gift to her, to know that you met Him before she passed, don't you?"

Henry did not answer. The look on his face told the story: How did I end up in this home, when all I wanted were directions to the right freeway to Houston?

"Do you have money?" Dad asked.

The man hung his head. When he had gotten the call about his mother, she had only a few days to live. He had used all his money to put gas in the car, with barely enough left over for another two or three tankfuls.

"Henry, don't worry. We'll help." Dad was in his element. He was an amazing multitasker who could keep five balls in the air and not miss a thing. "Ritalynn, go break open your piggy bank and search Daddy's pants pockets for change, then check your mother's purse. Carmen, do you have any change, or did you spend it at the game yesterday? Mother, I bought that new loaf of bread. Can you make two or three sandwiches with chips for Henry to have on the road? And give him some of those home-made chocolate chip cookies you made too. They're delicious."

I caught Mom's expression as she stood just out of sight in the kitchen. I had seen that same look many times before, most recently with Stephen, the homeless man. I remembered how that turned out.

Henry sat down at the dining room table while Mom served him the nice meal she spontaneously whipped up from ingredients she had on hand—hot tuna salad with pasta, fresh green beans and tomatoes, leftover Jell-O salad, fresh corn muffins, and a freshly brewed glass of iced tea. She amazed me with how quickly she could take a can of tuna and a box of pasta and turn it into a delicious dinner. (I learned from her to always keep essentials on hand when I had my own home, just in case I had to prepare a meal for a drop-in guest.)

In less than an hour, Henry had eaten a great meal and received a to-go meal that included two sandwiches, fruit, chips, and cookies in a Styrofoam cooler, plus iced tea in a thermos. I collected $50 cash from my piggy bank and other emergency stash, and Dad provided clear directions and maps to get him back to Houston.

But the greatest gift Henry received that night was when he prayed with Dad to receive Christ as his personal Savior. As he left our home that night, he said, "I thought following you was to find my way to Houston, but God had me find my way to Him. My mother is never going to believe this story."

Three days later, Henry called to let Dad know that his mother had passed away soon after he had arrived home. When he walked into her bedroom, she took one long look at his face and asked, "When did you find Jesus, son?" He shared the story of his encounter with Jesus when he followed a white family home in California, thinking that they would give him directions back to Houston. He received that and so much more.

Henry then shared her final words: "Henry, you experienced the real Jesus who longs to lavish upon us. I can now go home to Him. My prayers have been answered."

———

By the time I turned twelve, I had attended several Billy Graham Crusades and had heard Billy speak many times. I wasn't thrilled when Dad insisted that I come along with the family to Angel Stadium, where Billy was preaching for the 1969 Anaheim crusade. It was an overflow crowd, the largest yet for any event in the stadium's history. Because we were on Campus Crusade staff and because Dad knew Billy and the team, we were given reserved seats near the front of the stage, which was located by the Los Angeles Angels' home plate. I would have rather been at home with my friends, and in protest I intentionally left the seat vacant between Dad and me.

Mom and Dad's friend Cliff Barrows was leading the audience in song, and the choir was standing as Ted Innes and Ted Smith played the organ and piano. I had just settled into my stadium seat when I heard the hushed whispers and gasps from the ladies seated around me. Turning to see what the fuss was all about, I noticed a grungy, disheveled-looking man slowly making his way down the steps, pausing at each landing to search the rows for an empty seat.

His appearance was off-putting, if not a little intimidating. He was dressed in all black—worn leather pants, a sleeveless T-shirt, and a weathered leather vest. He was gaunt and his eyes were lifeless, with the lids partially closed and suggesting heavy drug use. I thought he was in the wrong place and wondered how he got past the ushers. Only reserved ticket-holders were allowed in this section. Before I knew it, he was standing next to my row, peering at the empty seat between Dad and me.

"We've been saving this for you!" Dad offered cheerfully.

As I stood to let him pass, the unmistakable stench of stale cigarette smoke, alcohol, and marijuana filled my nostrils. Dad did not seem to notice.

"Hi, my name is Lionel." Dad extended his hand. "What's yours?"

No response.

"I'm so glad you're here. Do you want a drink of water? It is warm out here, but it'll get better once the sun goes down." Without waiting for a reply, Dad placed a cold bottle of water in the man's hands, along with a bag of nuts.

He just stared back at Dad, expressionless.

Dad made several attempts to connect, all with no response. When we stood to sing, Dad held the paper songbook up to share. One of the guest speakers said something funny, and Dad looked over and smiled, trying to catch the man's eye. During Scripture reading, Dad held out his Bible to share.

As Billy delivered his message, the man nervously tapped his leg as fast as an auctioneer, occasionally sipping the water and eating a nut.

When the invitation was given, I kept my eyes focused straight ahead, secretly hoping Dad wouldn't say anything. But he was undaunted by the man's silence and unintimidated by his appearance. He turned to the man and asked if he wanted to know Jesus. The man slowly got to his feet but still said nothing. The next thing I knew, Daddy was leading him down to the field where people were gathering to pray.

Hours later, Dad learned the man's name was Rick Carreno and he was the fourth-highest-ranking leader in California's most notorious motorcycle gang, the Hells Angels. Rick's nickname was "Psycho." He had come to the crusade only out of respect for his mother, who had pleaded for him to attend one night. He promised to come but refused to sit with her. Out of defiance, he had jumped over the reserved gate, thinking that someone would surely try to stop him. Instead, he was offered a seat next to Dad.

Unbeknownst to us, Rick was a mainline heroin addict. When Dad bought him a hot dog after the crusade, it was the first bite of real food he had eaten in more than four days. Rick never went through heroin withdrawals. Instead, he experienced a supernatural transformation that night.

Before the night was over, Dad called Bill Bright to ask if he could bring Rick as his guest to Arrowhead Springs. Dad was convinced that, as a new believer, Rick needed to be surrounded by sharp kids his age who loved the Lord. Bill was hesitant at first, but Dad promised he would take personal responsibility for Rick, and Bill consented. After only a few days with the group at Arrowhead Springs, some of the youth complained that Rick's presence was intimidating, and he was asked to leave. Mom and Dad agreed take Rick into our home, and for the next two years he lived with our family.

Rick was a changed man, but he had a long journey ahead to "unlearn" years of abuse, neglect, and rejection. Dad stayed close by Rick's side, mentoring him in how to read the Word, how to hear from God, and how to trust Him. I witnessed the transformation in Rick, many times watching him kneel on the floor in worship and prayer. I heard him share what He had read in the Bible and what it had meant to him. His relationship with his mother blossomed, and he developed healthy friendships for the first time in his life.

In the 1960s, the Hells Angels were a much-feared "outlaw" biker gang, notorious for criminal activity, drugs, and intimidation. It was a 24/7 lifestyle, leaving the club was rarely achieved, and Rick's former motorcycle gang did not like his new life choice. One night I came home to find two strangers seated at our dining room table and the house reeking of marijuana. They were introduced as Skip and Cannibal, and both came from two other notorious motorcycle clubs: Satan's Slaves and the Outlaws. They had heard rumors that Rick had found religion, and wanted to see firsthand. Skip, Cannibal, and Rick had all grown up in the same Los Angeles neighborhood, but each had joined a different club.

Mom and Dad welcomed the bikers into our home, fixed a good meal for them, and Dad shared his testimony. After several hours of conversation, these motorcycle club members kneeled and invited Jesus into their lives. Dad persuaded each man to drink a glass of milk, most certainly the only milk they had consumed since childhood, and sent them off with a Bible and a bear hug.

As a newly transformed believer, Rick felt remorse for his past life and became convicted that he needed to turn himself in for a crime he had committed. But coming forward would also expose others. Dad supported Rick's decision, and found other believers to help financially in hiring top lawyers. He also sought out endorsements of Rick's character from Billy Graham, Bill Bright, and other well-known Christians to provide to the judge on Rick's case. The judge considered Rick's apology and his personal restitution, and ruled in Rick's favor.

When word of Rick's confession to the crime reached his old motorcycle gang, the leaders were fearful of being exposed and were furious—so much so that the Hells Angels put a "hit" on Rick as well as Dad. There had been no secrets revealed in Rick's court hearing, but that did not matter to the other leaders. No one left the Hells Angels and lived to tell about it.

It was Christmastime and our entire family, including Rick and his girlfriend, were enjoying the festivities at the Campus Crusade headquarters at Arrowhead Springs. Dad then received word that several bikers were riding up the back side of the mountain.

"Lionel," Bill Bright warned, "you need to stay in the hotel. Our security teams are on their way, and they have notified the sheriff and the police."

"I won't hear of it," Dad said. "This won't end until these bullies are faced. When they come, Rick, you stay here with Dr. Bright, and I'll go out and face them."

"Lionel, you can't!" Mom pleaded. "They may kill you."

But Dad's mind was made up. "Now, Dorothy, the Lord is with me just as He was with David. I come in the name of the Lord."

The loud Harley engines shook the hotel front lobby. I counted seven Hells Angels. Big, burly guys with cigarettes hanging from their mouths, tattoos covering each arm, and long hair pulled back under their helmets. Security had not arrived. I went around to a side door where I could see without being seen, while Dad walked boldly out the front door.

"Who's in charge?" he demanded.

The guy in back revved his motor in reply.

Dad walked over and stood eye to eye with him as he sat on his long hydraulic chopper. It looked just like the one in the movie *Easy Rider.* "You boys don't intimidate me. You're nothing more than a bunch of bullies trying to scare us."

When the leader stood up, he towered over Dad.

Standing his ground, Dad pointed his finger at the man's face. "You're a scared little kid who's probably never had a dad or someone close to you ever tell you that you were loved. So, will it make you feel big if you beat up a small old man like me? Is that what you want to do? Go ahead. I'm not afraid. But before you do, let me tell you that there is someone who loves you, and gave His life for you so that you would be free."

The guy sat back down on his motorcycle and laughed. He said something to others, and they drove away just as the police and security rounded the corner. Dad waved for the police and sheriff's deputies to stay back while the Hells Angels passed.

A few months later, Rick was cornered by a group of Hells Angels on a street in downtown Los Angeles. He was face-to-face with the men who wanted him dead. Two of the members drew their knives and tried to approach Rick, but they were supernaturally prevented from attacking him.

Rick went on to establish Rick Carreno Ministries, and neither he nor Dad ever encountered another threat.

———

After several years of handling special projects for Campus Crusade and serving as fill-in host for Bill Bright when he was out of town, Dad was asked to serve in the Military Ministry of Campus Crusade by its national director, Colonel John M. Fain (U.S. Air Force, Retired). Colonel Fain had a special "joint" assignment for Mom and Dad, and he readily admitted it wouldn't be an easy one.

Mom and Dad would disciple a highly decorated career military officer, Colonel Heath "Bo" Bottomly, and his wife, Beverly. The colonel had received Christ while serving in Vietnam but had not grown much in his faith. Dad had heard about him previously since the man's daughter was Dad's administrative assistant.

Colonel Bottomly was a West Point graduate, a career fighter pilot who had survived four wars. He had served in a wide variety of assignments in Washington and in several countries as a fighter pilot, base commander, United Nations peacekeeper, presidential advisor, Secretary to the Joint Chiefs of Staff, negotiator, and spy. He was given command of the largest and most powerful aggregate of fighting forces of any war, and had been decorated with many military honors. A tough man, he had been appropriately nicknamcd "Bald Eagle."

In his one introduction to Colonel Bottomly months earlier, Dad was quickly made aware of his accomplishments: "You know, Lionel, I mastered jet planes and commanded the first jet squadron in the Far East and was the first to fly across the Atlantic Ocean. I served on the Joint Chiefs of Staff during the Korean War and was a special intelligence observer during the Arab-Israeli war, and appointed to direct operations of the Nuclear Alert Force to the 81st Tactical Fighter Wing in Europe and North Africa."

The colonel's rank and demeanor were enough to intimidate almost anyone. He and Dad had nothing in common but their love for country and God. Dad had been awarded the rank of "honorary colonel" by former governor Lester Maddox of Georgia, but he had no credentials that would gain the respect of this man.

Still, Dad had a genuine love for people, and he was not about to be intimidated. Besides, he had been tamed by the love of the Savior. Early on in their relationship, the colonel used his military credentials to belittle my father. Instead of retaliating or becoming angry, Dad would counter back, "Colonel, do you know why the Lord made me five foot two? Had he made me six feet tall, I would have knocked your block off many times."

The colonel laughed it off, but he was still determined to get my father to react.

Mom began meeting with the colonel's wife for Bible study, and after meeting only a handful of times, Beverly accepted Christ as her personal Savior. As she grew in her faith, one by one, each of their five children had personal encounters with Jesus Christ. Our families became close, often sharing meals, Bible studies, and parties at each other's homes.

One chilly evening in November, our families had gathered around the Bottomly's swimming pool. The colonel was athletic, fit, and physically imposing, and without saying a word, he picked up Dad and threw him into the pool fully clothed.

Unfazed, Dad removed his shoes and trousers, treaded water, and leaned on the edge of the pool. "Colonel," he said, "is that the best you can do? I thought you could at least throw me into the center of the pool rather than into four feet of water! I'm greatly disappointed. Try again and see if you can do a little better."

The colonel approached to take him up on his challenge, but Beverly protested, "No, Bo. You'll kill him. Lionel's not a young man! Stop!"

The colonel backed off, but that exchange broke the ice between them. From then on, their relationship took on a new tone. Dad spent hours with the colonel, promoting speaking opportunities for him across Southern California. During these hours driving together, they studied the Word and shared what they were learning.

For thirty-three years, people had expressed total allegiance to Colonel Heath Bottomly. Dad stood tall despite his bullying tactics, and as the colonel grew in grace, he softened. What would have caused most men to fear, Dad faced. The colonel later said of their relationship, "Lionel, I love you. No other man could have ever loved my edges off. But God knew, and he chose you."

ICE CREAM AND JESUS

Y EARS (ALTHOUGH I'M UNSURE how many) after losing
our money and transitioning to Crusade staff, the playful-
ness, spontaneity, and fun that had characterized our family
life eventually returned to our home. Once Mom and Dad fully
grieved their financial loss and became accustomed to trusting
God for every ounce of provision, their new freedom brought
out a genuine joy and childlike abandon in their personalities
that attracted others like magnets.

Our home gained quite the reputation among neighbors,
classmates, Crusade staff, church friends, and even casual
acquaintances as the happening place. Spontaneous gatherings were common, as both Christian and non-Christian friends
dropped in throughout the evening to be part of the fun. Mom
learned to keep the food coming to accommodate the staggered
stream of people, and almost every night of the week had its
own special attraction. Friday night was taco night, Saturday
night was game night, and any night was ice cream night. Dad

developed a large following for his elaborately concocted ice cream sundaes, with guests even showing up at the door carrying their own bananas, board games, and sundae toppings.

These gatherings weren't evangelical outreaches, and no one felt preached to or forced to listen to the Four Spiritual Laws. My parents were people expressing the authentic love of Christ to others, and the talk about Jesus flowed as naturally and as freely as the ice cream. A couple who used to entertain the dignified air of high society, Mom and Dad were now more likely to instigate elaborate practical jokes and funny schemes that left guests holding their sides and snorting with raucous laughter. Like the time Dad's "Aunt Ethel" paid an unexpected visit during one of the nightly impromptu gatherings.

Dad had excused himself earlier in the evening, and before he returned, there was a dainty knock at the front door. Mom answered the door and graciously invited in the most awkward woman anyone had ever seen. She was of medium stature and stocky, wearing high heels and baggy nylons. Her dark hair covered her eyes and her red lipstick went well beyond her shapeless lips. Mom assisted the woman into the living room and introduced her to the rest of the guests as Lionel's aunt, Miss Ethel Burnham.

As the woman took each guest's hand and carried on a brief conversation, Mom called upstairs for Dad to come greet her. Aunt Ethel's voice quivered shyly as she punctuated her conversation with phrases like "my bra straps are killing me" and "my girdle is riding up."

After several minutes of polite conversation, one of the guests, the shyest and most inhibited young man in the room, suddenly burst out in laughter, pointing his finger at Aunt Ethel. The other guests recoiled at his rudeness until someone else caught on and squealed out in laughter while also pointing. Aunt Ethel pretended to be aghast at their lack of manners. Finally, someone blurted out, "Hey, everybody! Look at those hairy legs. That isn't Lionel's aunt. That's Lionel!"

With the joke now revealed, Dad pulled off the wig and attempted to stand in the high heels, but fell backward into his chair as he roared with laughter. One of the reasons people liked bringing their non-Christian friends to our house was that Mom and Dad broke the "stuffy" stereotype of being a Christian. And they didn't just break it, they redefined it.

Dad's love for Christ was contagious, and sharing it was such a natural part of who he was. On a flight from Denver to San Bernardino, he won a contest for being the oldest man on the flight. The prize was a bottle of champagne, but instead of accepting the champagne, Dad asked the flight attendant if he could share something that had changed his life. The attendant handed Dad the microphone. For the next forty-five minutes, he shared his testimony of how Jesus Christ was in the business of changing lives and loved to turn tragic pasts into triumphs. The flight ended with six first-time decisions for the Lord and several stronger commitments by Christians.

Mom and Dad looked for ways to extend love to people who were often overlooked or disdained. One such group of people were the garbage men. Each week they waited for the garbage men to make their rounds, and met them at the curb with a plate of homemade cookies and cold drinks. It was awkward for the men at first; they seemed a little skeptical. But Mom and Dad kept it up and eventually built relationships with them. They inquired about their families, and at Christmastime, Mom and Dad bought Christmas gifts for each of the garbage men's children.

The next year at Thanksgiving, Dad called the company and secured permission from their boss to be excused from work for one hour for a Thanksgiving dinner at our house. Dad escorted the four garbage men into our home, seated them around our dining room table, and he and Mom served them a full seven-course Thanksgiving dinner on china with sterling silver flatware. Three of the four men did not know Jesus, but that day, all four men left with Jesus in their hearts.

Another group of people they ministered to were the painters Dad hired to paint our house. We were still struggling to raise support and provide for basic needs, but neighbors complained that our house needed painting. Dad found two men who had experience and needed work, but they had just been released from prison. With references from a friend, Dad hired them to do the job. Night after night, their wives and children came to dinner and Mom and Dad shared their life stories of God's love.

Two weeks into the project, one of the guys told Dad that their truck was not going to last and they were in the market for a car. Dad quickly offered to lend them our Oldsmobile for the night as a trial, explaining that we were thinking of selling it and would give them a great price if they liked it. They agreed to let Dad know in the morning.

Mom was appalled. "Lionel, what were you thinking?" she said after they left. "They're ex-cons, and you may have just helped them steal our only car!"

"Mother darling, I'm not worried," he replied. "God is providing a new car for us, although we have no idea when or where."

"Exactly. You acted like you knew a car was lined up for us." Mom was not convinced.

"Dorothy, God has this. He has been faithful and never let us down. Let's pray."

The next day, the painters did not return with our car, nor did they call. We had no car. Not only that, but the paint job was only half finished.

For several days, we called on friends to take us grocery shopping and run errands, while Dad continued to assure us that God had this and He was faithful. One week after the painters stole our car, a friend from another state called and said that the Lord had impressed upon them to give us a car, and that they were driving their older car to California.

Two weeks after that, a summer staffer from Campus Crusade called and said he was starting a painting business and was looking for work to build his business. Within two months after the painters had taken our car, we had a "new" car in the garage and our home was completely painted. But that's not the end of the story.

The painters returned with our car and admitted that they had no intention of returning it, but the love and acceptance of my parents prevented them from keeping it. Mom and Dad shared how Jesus had taken care of us with a new car and a new painter, and Dad signed over to them the legal title to our old car. That night, Dad led the painters and their families to the Lord.

Mom and Dad loved pouring into others, and in time, their ministry developed into one that looked fundamentally different than it had when they were wealthy. Rather than "underwriting" others' ministries financially, they had their own ministry, one that reached beyond important "movers and shakers" to include ordinary people.

They began hosting a Bible study at Campus Crusade that grew to over one hundred and fifty attendees. Mom started leading the women's ministry in Palm Springs and soon had over five hundred women involved in learning more about God, with over a dozen study groups spread throughout the city. Dad was often called on to preach on Wednesday evenings in Palm Springs or share his testimony in CBMC meetings.

They returned to entertaining in our home as they once enjoyed, which sometimes put a strain on limited finances, especially on one Thanksgiving. Dad convinced Mom that he and Carmen could handle prepping and stuffing the twenty-four-pound turkey she had purchased for a dinner party, and arranged for Mom to spend the afternoon at the beauty salon getting her hair and nails done for the evening.

Unable to find a mixing bowl big enough for the stuffing, Dad cleaned and disinfected the kitchen sink and dumped all the chopped-up ingredients into it. He began mixing the ingredients together, and water from the dishwasher suddenly backed up into the sink. It dislodged the drain plug, bubbling up into the stuffing and then sucking it down the disposal. With quick thinking, Carmen and Dad rescued as much stuffing as they could but were left with a soggy mess.

To make matters worse, and to "save" the dinner from ruin, Dad added rye bread to the mix to soak up the excess water, which worked like a charm. The turkey was stuffed, sewn together, and cooking in the oven when Mom returned from the salon. The house smelled like Thanksgiving dinner should smell, and there was no telltale evidence of the dishwater dressing disaster.

Dad probably would have gotten away with it had Carmen not innocently spilled the beans by whispering, "Are you going to tell her what happened?"

With Dad's secret exposed, Mom could not be convinced to serve it to unsuspecting guests, so Dad got busy finding forty-five precooked Cornish game hens. Mom stalled dinner until he returned, but he aroused suspicion carrying in so many containers past the guests in the living room. To her horror, he confessed the whole story of the stuffing to the dinner guests. The room erupted with laughter, and it became a legend around Campus Crusade.

Whatever Mom and Dad did, they did as a team. Long before the "women's movement," we had no traditional gender roles in our home. Dad ran the vacuum while Mom put the dishes away after a dinner party, or vice versa. At Christmastime, when we made hundreds of pounds of fudge as a family, Dad individually wrapped each piece, packed the boxes, and handwrote notes of encouragement to each family. Long after the crowds were gone from our house, I could hear Dad verbally affirm his love and support for Mom and her gifts.

Growing up in my home imparted to me that being a Christian should be a life of joy, fun, laughter, and creativity. I learned that it is perfectly acceptable to mix your personality with the gospel—and to mix ice cream and Jesus.

THE FATHER'S HEART

M OST TEENAGERS GO THROUGH a period when their parents aren't considered "cool," and I was no different. My time of this probably lasted longer than most people's, and if I could find a way to needle Dad, I did. Dad certainly wasn't perfect, but most of the time he responded in a way that pointed me to the One he knew intimately, his Father in heaven.

As I stood in front of my junior high school, laughing and talking with friends one day, Dad pulled up and cheerfully greeted us. Reluctant and a little embarrassed, I jumped into the car.

Dad began to drive the opposite way home, which miffed me. "Why are you going this way?" I asked.

He looked over at me. "I thought we would get ice cream."

"I just want to go home."

He ignored me and instead stopped to get us both a vanilla cone, then drove the gradual incline up the mountain.

I slumped in my seat.

Daddy smiled and remarked how delicious the ice cream tasted.

I just wasn't into it.

Abruptly, he pulled over on the side of the highway. "Ritalynn, look at this beautiful field of flowers!"

He jumped out of the car and, halfheartedly, I followed. He remarked how excited he was to explore something together with his daughter. Stooping down, he picked up a broken piece of fence and then pried the rusty barbed wire apart just far enough for me to crawl through. "This is so beautiful, isn't it?" he said. "Look at these stunning purple flowers! There are so many! They look like velvet."

I returned his enthusiasm with silence, annoyed that we had driven all the way up here just to see a field of flowers. Then his eye caught something I had failed to see. He leaned over and picked up one little yellow flower, alone among all the purple ones. "Wow, honey. Look at how special this flower is. There's no other flower like it." He looked me in the eye, held out the flower, and gently said, "Ritalynn, *you* are this yellow flower. You stand out in a crowd. You are one of a kind, yet you spend so much time trying to fit in when you are created to stand out. You have no need to compare yourself to anyone else."

Daddy knew me well. He saw the insecurities of my heart and my struggle with self-image. When I displayed anger and frustration, he looked deep into my soul to see the beauty of the scared little girl inside—the girl who desperately needed to know she was valued and one of a kind.

That's the way Dad viewed everyone he met, in a way that they would know they were greatly loved, highly valued, and accepted. In fact, he was known for always asking three questions: First, has anyone told you today that they love you with all of their heart? Second, has anyone told you that you could do all that God has for you today? Without waiting for an answer, he would tell them that he loved them, and they could do everything that God had for them because He was right there as a guarantee. Then he would ask the third question: How has God proven that to you today?

He always waited for this response, and wouldn't budge until he was given a good answer—or three. Almost every day for as long as I can remember, he raced home in the afternoon to go through this routine with me when I got home from school. It was annoying at times, especially when I struggled to find enough specific answers that would satisfy him, even if it meant making them up. Honestly, sometimes I was just trying to get him to quit asking. A typical exchange sounded something like this.

> Dad: "How has God proven today that He loves you?"
> Rita: "I got an A on my test."
> Dad: "What time was that test?"
> Rita: "About eight this morning."
> Dad: "Ritalynn, that was eight. It's now three forty-five. What else?"

I didn't appreciate it then, but that simple routine established a foundation for recognizing the Father's presence and His heart for me. It taught me to be always looking for and expecting God's activity in my life. Likewise, as I have met others who knew Dad, they too have shared the profound impact of those three questions.

Even when Dad made mistakes, as parents do, he was humble enough to admit it and ask for forgiveness. I struggled during my teenage years to get God to "do things" for me the way I thought

He did for Dad. Even at an early age, I wanted the kind of relationship Dad had with God, but every time I tried, I seemed to fall short. In my frustration, I once told Dad I hated him and not to talk to me about "his" Jesus. I pushed Dad aside and stormed upstairs to my room, but he followed me in angry pursuit.

"Ritalynn, we have done everything we know to do. We have run out of ideas to help you. You can't talk to your father this way." He took off his belt.

I knew I had pushed too far, but I didn't care. "Go ahead, old man. See what you can do." I was horrified by my own words. It would have escalated badly had Mom not intervened.

"Both of you, stop right now. This is not going anywhere, and Lionel, you must be at a Campus Crusade banquet tonight to emcee for Bill Bright. Ritalynn, you're coming too. It's expected."

The last place I wanted to be that night was the banquet, especially with my parents. Refusing to sit with Mom and Dad, I chose a seat in the back of the room. The auditorium was packed with summer staff. Outwardly I was still fuming, but inside I was desperately looking for something to justify my behavior. I couldn't.

Dad, in his seventies, walked slowly to the platform without his usual pep. "Before I can do anything tonight,"—Dad's voice cracked—"I have to make something right between my precious daughter Ritalynn and me. We had an unfortunate exchange between us, and I allowed the Enemy to get the best of me and I said some things that exasperated her and added fuel to the fire. Ritalynn, wherever you are, forgive your old man for not loving you right. I know better. There is nothing in this world your mother and I would not do for you. Forgive me."

The crowd was silent. I wanted to run. Not run away, but run to him and fall into his arms, but I couldn't. Instead I walked away.

Often, I was the one who needed to be forgiven but was the last one to ask. Dad always forgave me, always pursued me, just like the father pursued the prodigal son. His actions taught me a lot about how it feels to be forgiven, even when you're the one who deserves anything but.

Beyond forgiving me, Dad took great personal interest in everything that was important to me, even if it meant great personal risk for him. He knew I was searching spiritually, and understood how I might be drawn to the emotional appeal of a charismatic church (as opposed to the intellectual approach of Campus Crusade). After all, he had explored Aimee Semple McPherson's message back when he was a younger man.

When I became interested in attending Greg Laurie's church, Calvary Chapel Riverside, Dad wanted to go with me to encourage me in my walk. But going to Calvary Chapel presented a big problem: Campus Crusade policies forbid staff members from attending charismatic churches. By doing so, staff could risk losing their position and their supporters.

Dad was more interested in me, and what God was doing in my life, than following a policy. He went with me to Calvary Chapel on a Sunday night, sat close to the front, and was engaged with the singing and followed closely when the message was preached. I was proud he was with me, but what happened afterward meant even more.

"Ritalynn," Dad affirmed, "I understand why you love this church, and as far as I'm concerned, you need to continue going wherever you're growing. I'll make an appointment with Bill

Bright and tell him. Besides, his son attends, and Bill might want to visit himself."

Dad did make an appointment with Bill, and he graciously affirmed Dad's decision. In fact, it became the very encouragement for Bill Bright that bridged the gap with his own son.

When I was captain of my high school tennis team, Dad sat for hours in the hot California sun to watch me hit balls against the backboard, just to keep me company. I was named most valuable player in the region, and I believed tennis was going to be my career, until I injured my knee enough times that it ruined my chances of getting a tennis scholarship to UCLA. Then, Dad was the one who encouraged me to let God have my every dream.

I continued to play competitively when I started Biola University, and was close to making the cut for the tennis team when I re-injured my knee, this time more severely than the others. The ER doctor told me I would never play competitive tennis again. In the emergency room, heartbroken, I called my giant—Dad. He dropped everything he was doing and drove the seventy miles from San Bernardino to Biola.

He made calls to everyone he knew who might point him to the best orthopedic doctor in California. With a referral to the team orthopedic physician for the Los Angeles Rams and the University of Southern California Trojans, he was able to get me an appointment within a few days. Dad never let me out of his sight, following me into the examination room.

I had damaged the main nerves in my leg and chipped my knee cap in several locations. The cartilage had deteriorated from frequent dislocations, and the tendons needed to be cut and tied. The new doctor told me I might never be able to walk again, much less play tennis. I couldn't move my toes, and my left leg felt numb from the knee down.

Dad held me as he prayed. He thanked God in everything, as we are taught in Philippians 4:6: "Do not be anxious about anything, but in everything by prayer and supplication with thanksgiving, let your requests be made known to God" (ESV). He held me in his arms that night and explained that we don't thank God for the bad, but we trust Him that He is greater than the situation.

A few days later, we were at the specialist in Hollywood. They took x-rays, and the doctor confirmed that I would never play tennis again. I left discouraged, but Dad held on to his faith, not allowing anything to destroy his trust in the all-powerful, sovereign God, his Savior and Lord, Jesus Christ. He assured me that he would be by my side during the long road of rehabilitation. A year later, with swimming and physical therapy, my leg was healed, but I never played competitively again.

Just as the Father loves to lavish on His children, Dad enjoyed surprising me with the desires of my heart. When my old Volkswagen Beetle (nicknamed Herbie) became unreliable, he and Mom drove all over Southern California searching for the car of my dreams. I wasn't very appreciative of their sacrifice, and I certainly displayed my annoyance when he handed me what appeared to be the keys to a model I hated.

"Rita, sweetheart, I love you," he said. "I got you a car, precious. You'll love it."

"Dad, how could you?" I protested. "I can't see out of that one without a pillow!"

Just then, the salesman stepped out of a brand-new 1976 Datsun B210 hatchback. It had only been driven two miles, and the seats were still wrapped in plastic. "Congratulations!" he said. "You're a new car owner!"

I was speechless. And ashamed. Dad had wanted me to have a nicer and sportier car, a Datsun 240Z, but I wanted a hatchback. He had listened to what I wanted, after all. I hugged him as tears rolled down his cheeks. It was as if he had never heard all my complaining and hateful words.

Sometimes, it was the creative little things Dad did that expressed his heart of love. For the three years I was away at boarding school in Florida, I received a handwritten note from him every single day. One of the most unforgettable letters was one written on a circular paper coaster, with the letters printed neatly around in circles using several different colors of ink. Sometimes he drew cartoons in his letters, but he always had a message from God's Word that addressed a question I had about God.

When we are children, our initial understanding of what a marriage should be like is the one patterned by our parents. Even before I knew what to look for, I saw how Dad treated Mom. He was a student of her in the sense that he knew the little things that would make her feel honored as a woman and equal as a partner. Today, we would say he "spoke her love language."

He made her breakfast most mornings, and often throughout the day he would call just to tell her he loved and appreciated her. Even after twenty years of marriage, he made "dates" with her, then shopped for a new outfit for her and had it delivered to the house with a note that said, "Darling, be ready at 6:30." He encouraged her to go out with her friends, and made appointments for her to get her hair and nails done. He sent her flowers for no reason other than to say "I love you."

As kids do, I sometimes thought it was a little corny, but in reality, it created an expectation that this is the heart of God for His children and that one day I would want a husband who would love me like this.

One of the creative letters from Dad

HOMEGOING

EVEN AT SEVENTY-NINE, DAD had more energy than most men half his age. Slowing down was not in his DNA. He routinely kept twelve-hour days, and maintained a disciplined approach to life that he had practiced so many years in business. Each day started before dawn, with his awakening to spend the most important part of his day with the Lord. After that, a thirty-minute callisthenic workout. I could hear the grunts and groans from my room.

A few minutes after his shower, like clockwork, he would call my name. "Ritalynn, come see if your daddy is cool for his little girl! Does your daddy look sharp? Do you like this shirt with this tie?"

I always waited for that call. I enjoyed picking out shirts and ties for him, and thought it was cute that he always wanted my opinion and wanted me to be proud to be seen with him. As he and Mom made breakfast, he would joyfully rattle off the events on his calendar for the day—always packed full with service to others. "I'm taking Colonel Bottomly to a luncheon in Riverside to share his testimony with some military men. Later in the afternoon, Commander Harvey and I are visiting some veterans at the VA hospital, and tonight, don't forget that I give the message at church in Palm Springs."

Not long after his seventy-ninth birthday, he began to talk about his eightieth birthday. I thought it unusual for him to plan anything where the attention would be focused on him, but he loved parties, and turning eighty seemed to represent a significant milestone for him.

At night around the dining room table, Mom and Dad would talk excitedly about the old friends they would love to see again, people whose lives and ministries Dad had impacted over the years. It would be a joyful celebration, and Bill and Vonette Bright eagerly volunteered to host the event at the Arrowhead Springs Hotel, Campus Crusade headquarters.

After months of planning, the long-awaited birthday-celebration day finally arrived. I was in my first year of college at Biola University, about an hour away, but was happy to drive home for the big event. Going to formal banquets was a normal part of life for me, but I was truly looking forward to this one. As the hundreds of guests poured into the hotel that evening, the main Candlelight Ballroom quickly filled to capacity and overflowed into the adjacent ballroom.

The mood was festive, the room buzzing with the laughter and conversation of friends who hadn't seen each other in years. It was like Old Home Week, with prominent evangelical leaders assembled from across the country to honor Dad. Among them were Cy Nelson, founder of Gospel Light Publishing; former Youth for Christ leader Roy McKeown; Bob Pierce, founder of

World Vision and Samaritan's Purse; Dad's Occidental College roommate and pastor Louis Evans Sr.; Pat Zondervan, cofounder of Zondervan Publishing; gospel singers Stuart and Suzy Hamblen; and of course, Bill Bright. I flitted around the room, hobnobbing with Mom and Dad's good friends. I was proud of my daddy, and I wanted to be right with him.

Prior to taking the podium, the master of ceremonies canvassed each family member looking for "Lionel stories," both funny and poignant, that would capture Dad's personality. He told of Dad dressing up as Santa Claus every Christmas, and reading the Christmas story from the big family Bible before opening presents. He mentioned family parties with taffy pulls, popcorn balls, and Daddy's intricately layered salads of many colors. And of course, his famous hot fudge sundaes. On a more serious note, he read one of Dad's love letters to Mom, artfully worded and beautifully touching, penned to her after twenty years of marriage.

Throughout the evening, testimonies, tributes, laughter, and singing celebrated Dad's impact on each speaker's life. He was finally getting the recognition I always thought he deserved. At eighteen, I soaked it all in, and with each testimony, God stirred my desire for a life that would impact others the way Dad's had.

Roy McKeown shared the following about Dad:

> When I first met Lionel Mayell, I was tremendously confused about him. Winston Churchill said it best: "To me he was a riddle wrapped in an enigma." By chance I became acquainted with him, although he maintains that there is no such thing as a "happen-chance"—each event is planned by God. I can truly say

now, after knowing him for a couple of decades, that the latter must be true, for he has had an influence upon my life unequalled by any man. He speaks what he lives, and lives what he speaks.

Someone once asked Francis of Assisi how he was able to accomplish so much. He replied, "This may be why. The Lord looked down from heaven and said, 'Where can I find the weakest, littlest man on earth?' Then He saw me and said, 'I've found him. I will work through him, and he won't be proud of it. He'll see that I'm only using him because of his insignificance.'"

When I took over as the West Coast director of Youth for Christ, Lionel was on the board. I was young, inexperienced, eager, and in need of a lot of love, help, guidance, and direction. And something else—money. Lionel stood with us. I'll never forget the first ride we had with him. There was Lionel, looking through the steering wheel trying to see the road, and there we were in the backseat. My wife said, "I have never been with a driver like this in my life. He can't see out."

But we arrived unscathed at the banquet. Lionel approached me afterward and said that he wanted me to know that he loved me and would support me in my ministry "until Jesus returns." That's the way he talks.

I don't know why I have been so honored to have a friend like him, but I am grateful and extremely humbled to have had the opportunity to have Lionel and Dorothy as my friends all these years.

Not many months after Dad's eightieth birthday, on my week-end trips home from Biola, I noticed some changes in his health. One afternoon I found him unsteady on his feet, even staggering as he walked across the living room. He had not heard me come in the house, and I ran to his side and grabbed him to prevent a fall. Then he whispered, "Don't tell your mother, Ritalynn." I kept our secret, but I watched him more attentively.

A few weeks later, when the semester was over and I was home on break, Dad and I went on errands together. As we drove, the car came awfully close to the curb. "Daddy, you're going to hit the curb," I said.

"Oh no, Ritalynn. I have it," he assured me.

I knew in my heart he was hiding something. Over lunch, I pressed him for the truth. He finally shared that he had glau-coma and was blind in one eye. Again, he asked me not to say anything to Mom; he did not want to worry her.

By the end of summer, things had gotten worse. Carmen was in the dining room talking with a friend, planning their trip to Dallas for their first year in seminary. Mom, Dad, and I were all chiming in on their discussion, when I noticed something was not right with Dad.

"Daddy, your coloring looks poor," I said.

Carmen took Dad's pulse, then told Mom to get the car so we could go to Loma Linda Hospital. Ray, Carmen's friend, manu-ally lifted our garage door while Carmen and I helped Dad into the car. Carmen kept his finger on Dad's pulse as Mom raced to Loma Linda and I sat silently next to Dad.

When Mom pulled into the emergency room's circular drive-way, attendants rushed out to get Dad, then wheeled him through the double doors. I followed the stretcher carrying Dad while Carmen and Ray helped Mom. Somehow I was able to sneak past the swinging doors, and I could see through the glass as the doctors applied paddles to Dad's chest.

Later on, in ICU, the doctors conferred with Mom, Carmen, and me. Dad had a heart condition that had been diagnosed years earlier when he slid off the road and down an embankment on his way to Campus Crusade. During the checkup after the accident, the doctors discovered Dad had coronary artery disease, or hardening of the arteries. This was during the 1970s, and treatment for coronary artery disease was not as advanced as it is now. Carmen and I were in high school at the time, and Dad didn't want us to know.

Suddenly, the pieces of the puzzle started to make sense. When I was home on weekends, I had noticed Mom giving Dad a tiny pill with his banana each morning. It was nitroglycerin, a medication used to dilate arteries that have been narrowed by atherosclerosis. It never occurred to me to ask what the pill was for. Now I knew why Dad had been so fixated on his eightieth birthday and why he wanted to spend every moment with us. It was a milestone. For him.

Dad remained in the hospital for several days. On his fourth day there, Mom announced that she and Carmen had to drive to Palm Springs for a banquet. "We need to do these things to maintain our support," she explained to me. "We can't afford not to go."

I hated support-raising and the obligation and burden that my mother felt. Now didn't seem like the time to leave Dad and raise support. When I arrived on the cardiology floor, the nurses were laughing and talking about a man who had tried to escape. It came as no surprise to me that that man was Dad.

He wanted so badly to be home that he had mustered enough strength to get dressed and make it past the nurses' station and down the elevator. As he hailed a taxi, a hospital attendant noticed his slippers. Busted. Dad had not had the strength to put on his shoes.

He was on the bed crying when I arrived. "Ritalynn, please take me home."

My giant wanted to go home. And I was going to make that happen.

When Mom and Carmen got back from the banquet, I told them the story and insisted we bring Dad home. The next day, after agreeing to attentive care and weekly nursing visits, we did just that.

Dad gained strength every day and bounced back from that episode. Against the advice of the doctors, he resumed his work schedule at Campus Crusade. If he cut his pace any, it was just a little. Dad encouraged Carmen to go as planned to Dallas Seminary, and I went back to Biola. Mom seemed to be trying to convince herself that things were back to normal, but I knew in my heart that Dad was not 100 percent.

At the time of my twentieth birthday in November, I could see in Dad's eyes that he didn't feel well. From time to time, he would wink at me as if to say, "This is *our* secret." The next spring, not long after his eighty-first birthday in February, I had an extended spring break from Biola due to some stupid decisions I made that violated school policy. I took this opportunity to spend extra time alone with Dad, who was much weaker and spending many hours in bed.

I would not leave his side. I stroked his hand and brow, sang hymns to him, and read the Bible aloud. He would perk up when I read the Word, and the twinkle would return to his soft-blue eyes. One of his favorite old hymns I would sing was "Softly and Tenderly Jesus Is Calling."

"Ritalynn, Daddy is going home soon," he whispered as I sang it.

At first, I thought he might be confused, because he already was home. Then I realized he was speaking of his forever home—heaven.

Even when Dad wasn't feeling well, he still wanted to surprise Mom, his precious White Rosebud, on Mother's Day. Florist shops were closed since it was Sunday, but he assured me that God knew the situation and He would have a florist shop that would answer the phone. Daddy had me bring the phone from the dining room and plug it into the extension in his room, then sitting up in bed, he opened the phonebook and began dialing every florist. Several calls later, an owner answered. He ordered a dozen white roses for Mom, and I drove to the florist and picked them up so Dad could present them to her himself.

By July, his condition had worsened to the point that he couldn't walk at all and had great difficulty finding enough strength to speak. Dottie and Carmen came home to spend time with him. For the last several months, just Mom and I had been taking care of Dad, and it was hard to share the time with anyone else.

We had this secret handshake in our family—one person would clasp the other's hand and squeeze three times to spell out "I love you." The other person responded by squeezing two times, which was asking "how much?" The first person would squeeze five times, meaning "with all of my heart!" I knew Daddy wanted to speak, so I often practiced the family handshake with him so he could communicate to me.

Friends stopped by the house to pay their respects that summer, with increasing frequency. No one ever verbalized it, but we all seemed to know what was happening. Mom was encouraged by the fellowship of those who brought food or offered to run errands, but each visit only reminded me that the time I had left with Daddy was short.

It was difficult to see my giant dwindle. His days were characterized by exhausting gasps for breath. The life was draining from his body. He had sores, he didn't want solid food, and he spoke few words. Was this God's dynamo? For days without sleep, we all nursed Dad. His emaciated face had a contagious glow that revealed his soul. I couldn't leave his side; something other than death held me there.

Seeing the end of Daddy's life draw closer was so painful. We all took turns lifting him to the bathroom, and he was now only sipping liquids through a straw. It was my turn to stay up with him all night, and Mom had fallen asleep on the couch from exhaustion. I heard Dad gasping for air, and when I rushed into his room, he sat straight up in bed without any difficulty and pointed at something I could not see.

"Who's that beautiful man in white?" Dad's face was radiant, his voice clear and strong. "Ritalynn, he's right here. Don't you see him? He just told me it won't be long."

I could not speak or even move. The experience so unnerved me, I felt I had to get away. I did not know how to deal with Dad's death. He was my giant, my hero.

A friend and I drove to San Francisco for a few days, and when I returned, Dad could no longer talk. My friends challenged me to ask God to restore his voice. I had seen Dad ask God for "impossible" things many times before, and I had seen God answer him. That night I prayed and asked (really, I begged) God for a gift—to let me hear Dad's voice one more time. I knew in my spirit He would answer.

Two days later, I was alone with Dad while Mom, Dottie, and Carmen were out together on errands. To give Daddy a change of scenery, I used the lamb's wool underneath him to roll him onto a chaise lounge chair, then I pushed him into the living room. He seemed to enjoy being in the brighter room, and he smiled weakly and relaxed as he took in the sunshine. I sat down at the piano and began to play and sing, but when I tried to hit a really high note, my voice cracked and I screeched instead.

"Rita honey, breathe through your diaphragm," Dad said just above a whisper.

I swung the piano stool around as all the tears of the last four days and all of the unspoken fears and words gushed out all at once. "Oh, Daddy, you spoke to me! Oh, thank you, God! Thank you!" I told him how sometimes I struggled to know God but that I thought he was walking with me. Any other time, I might have responded to his correction with a smart-alecky comment, but I had just been given the greatest gift, and I needed to unload what was on my heart.

"Shhhh. I know you, honey. I know." Dad reached over and placed his hand over mine. "God has such wonderful blessings for you. It's so good. You're going to impact so many. If giving my life will turn you around more quickly, I gladly give my life. You are like your daddy. I know."

Daddy did know. He knew me well.

Just as he was finishing his blessing over me, my mother opened the door and she, too, heard his voice one more time.

That night was Mom's turn to sit with Dad through the night. She spent the time praying, reading the Bible to him, and assuring him of God's love as she did every night. The next morning, she reminded me to stop in and see him before I left on errands. Carmen and Dottie had been with him that morning and had just left his room moments earlier.

As I entered his room, I sensed something was different. He was motionless, his eyes open wide as if they had been fixed on something, or Someone. A look of awe animated his face. Somehow, I knew that this holy moment had been orchestrated just for me.

I had always said that I did not want to be near Dad when he died. At twenty, I was scared of death. But in this moment I felt no fear. I was witnessing a peek of glory. Daddy had locked eyes with Jesus. It was 11:15 a.m. on August 31, 1978.

I recalled what Daddy had said to me less than twelve hours earlier, that he would gladly give his life if it would turn me to Jesus more quickly. I had been the one to find him. Not my mother, not my sister or my brother. This was my moment to see. God stopped the world and chose the broken, imperfect, prodigal daughter to see a glimpse of heaven. God valued *me*.

I stood there for a few moments, taking it all in, before telling the others. Dad had been my protector, my cheerleader, my confidant, my giant. He had been the one person in the family who understood me when no one else did. But Dad had a closeness with Jesus—a trust and friendship I was hungry for and yet was missing from my experience.

I knew that this was God gently whispering to me that He wanted that relationship with me too. And in the stillness of that moment, I prayed aloud the words that God had been longing to hear from me: "God, I want everything and more that my daddy had. No matter what the cost." I wanted it all.

It was almost as if I felt Dad handing me over to the care of God. I was already saved. But that day I gave God permission to father me. I trusted Him with my life. It changed the way I viewed Him, and became the catalyst that launched me into the vibrant relationship with God that has shaped my life.

———

My journey has not been Dad's journey. I had to find my own relationship with God, and make my own mistakes along the way. But Dad's ultimate gift to me was giving me hope that God wanted to be an active part of every moment of my life, to share in it. His life taught me that God was in the everyday, that He cared about the little things, and that nothing was too big or too small. He taught me that I was valued, loved, one of a kind, and the apple of God's eye. His three questions were life-changing for me as an adult, and asking those questions is a practice I have used to change the lives of countless others I have counseled. Dad imparted the belief in my heart that I could be anything I wanted to be, that no dream of mine was too big for God. And that if I would let Him, God would use me to change the world too.

Yes, there was a giant in the land, and his name was Lionel Mayell.

Dad and me at his 80th birthday

AUTHOR'S NOTE

As people read *5'2" Giant, Builder of Dreams*, they inquired how I knew so much detail of my dad's story.

When I was seventeen, God planted a desire in my heart to write about my father's life. It became a dream that I could never let go of. With that dream came an unwavering faith that only grew over time. Perhaps in the beginning it was more about my need to see Daddy gain notoriety for the things he did that were hidden behind someone or something more famous. Later, I realized that wasn't the story at all. Rather, it was about an ordinary man who tapped into the dream of God and, with a God-sized faith, overcame obstacles and challenges and set his world on fire with the love of Jesus Christ.

Three months prior to my dad's death, I began recording his life story on cassette tapes. After his homegoing, as I went through his office, I found his personal notes of his life story. Perhaps he carried a desire to share it. I believe that dream was passed on to me.

I have faced the discouragement of having this manuscript verbally accepted by traditional publishers, only to be rejected later because they felt I didn't have a celebrity name that would generate sufficient sales. But when God gives you a dream, it doesn't matter what anyone says, it will happen—but only in His way and in His time.

During the years of waiting, praying, rewriting, and maturing, I continued to meet people whom my dad's life had impacted by leaving a legacy to believe God's love. I wish I could tell you that this dream quickly fell into place, but it didn't. I was discouraged by naysayers who said it was a waste of time, but along the way, God gave me markers of encouragement to anchor me with a hope and expectancy that rose above the many delays and discouragement. One such marker was when, during a major life transition, I placed everything I owned in storage for nine years. At the end of that time, I discovered that almost all my belongings had been ruined by black mold as a result of a major leak in the storage unit. There was one box that wasn't touched by the leak, and inside was this manuscript, *5'2" Giant.*

In 2015, I began to work on the manuscript again after a second traditional publisher voiced concern that the message was outdated. I rewrote the book from a different angle, completing the third rewrite. I spent hundreds of hours researching Dad's name and projects on the internet, contacting his building management companies, transcribing his tapes into Word documents, and researching his genealogy on Ancestry.com and MyHeritage.com.

I found my parents' written testimonies from the early days of Campus Crusade for Christ, my mom's journal and her wedding notes, and my dad's journal and dozens of his letters and writings about his life. I researched the history of California, the early days of building, and the National Register of Historic Places documents, and contacted UCLA, USC, Stanford, and Occidental to verify his transcripts (yes, they are still on file). I have dozens of original brochures of my dad's building projects, original photographs, and scrapbooks containing hundreds of articles and features from the 1940s, 1950s, and 1960s on Dad and his developments. My journey uncovered thousands of documents, and mentions of my dad in other books, building trade journals, newspapers, and magazines. Audio recordings of his involvement in the 1949 Los Angeles Crusade are on file in the Wheaton College Library Billy Graham Center Archives. This book has been researched and documented for accuracy.

I pray as you read this book, you too will embrace the hand of God in your own lives. I want you to have hope no matter what difficulty or circumstances you have encountered. As a little David standing before Goliath, Dad stood boldly in the face of what would seem to be insurmountable problems. Like David, he dreamed he could accomplish much, knowing and believing in a great personal, living God, his Lord and Savior Jesus Christ. He knew that in Christ all things *are* possible.

The hand of God was always manifested in the life of my father, although it was not always recognized. You too may not recognize God's hand in your life, but He is there for you as well. May this story rekindle hope and stir in you the flames of God's desires and the ability to dream His dreams, the best ones He has always had for you.

It was once said, "He who gives a good book gives more than cloth, paper, and ink ... more than leather, parchment, and words. He reveals a foreword of his thoughts, a dedication of his friendship, a page of his presence, a chapter of himself, and an index of his love" (author unknown). My hope is that you will discover, through Dad's story, the One who is love and brings lasting hope, and who desires to underwrite your story and enable you to change your world too.

ACKNOWLEDGMENTS

I would be remiss if I did not give Connie Day huge credit for helping me give voice to my dad's story, *5'2" Giant, Builder of Dreams*. She was there to assist me in research of the manuscript and treated it as if it were her own. I could not have asked for a better person to walk with me, encourage me, share my enthusiasm, and offer her amazing writing and editing skills. She has been my friend for over thirty years and faithfully encouraged me to believe this dream came from God and to take the next step, walking with me along the way. She knew exactly when I needed a break or a pep talk. Thank you. You embody the term *friend*.

Thank you to my prayer team who purposefully prayed for me, sent Scripture, and spoke Christ's life over me at the time I needed to be refreshed. I could count on you to listen and empathize in my struggles, celebrate with me, quietly pray, and sometimes boldly declare. You are handpicked by God, and I am eternally grateful for your unconditional love, wisdom, and friendship. Thank you, Susan Hayes and Grace Phillips.

I thank God for my friends who listened as I read and re-read chapters and repeatedly asked for their input. Thank you, Victoria Manley, Leslie Hunter, and Laura Haigler, for always encouraging me to take another step and undergirding me with your faith and prayers.

I am thankful for other supportive friends who faithfully inquired and prayed for me, encouraged me and stood with me through thick and thin.

I could not close without thanking my family: my brother Carmen, my sister and brother-in-law Dottie and Lowell Hartkorn. Thank you for your love, prayers, and for many of the memories we share in this book. I am so blessed you are my family.

Thank you to the team of professionals God brought together, whose tireless and conscientious work created a quality book that represents excellence. They are:

Christy Distler, Avodah Editorial Services, whose editorial prowess went above and beyond excellence.

Tim Green and Faceout Design Studio, whose creative genius captured the essence of *5'2" Giant.*

Kimberly Martin and the Jera Publishing team, who taught me about the world of publishing and provided layout for the book and logo design for Dunamai Press.

To the dozens of people who willingly read my book, gave helpful suggestions, and endorsed and encouraged me in this dream.

To all, I simply and lovingly say thank you!

ABOUT THE AUTHOR

As a transition expert and career strategist, Rita Mayell has coached hundreds of executives and emerging leaders, inspiring them to clarify purpose, discern God's timing, and move forward with conviction and strategic direction. Her career spans twenty-five-plus years as a transition coach, lay counselor, and executive search consultant, and she holds a Life and Leadership Certification in coaching and a Professional Coaching Certification (PCC) with the International Coaching Federation. A graduate of Biola University with a BA in Communications, a minor in Bible, and an emphasis in Psychology, she currently serves as Human Resources Strategist with Samaritan's Purse. She resides in Atlanta, Georgia, with four cats and one dog, all rescues with a story to tell.

If you were inspired by *5'2" Giant, Builder of Dreams* and are interested in learning more how you too can change your world, please visit: RitaMayell. com. Or if you are interested in Rita speaking for your group or conference, please go to: RitaMayell. com and click on **speaking**.

Connect with Rita on:

Facebook:	fb.me/RitaMayell
Twitter:	@RitaMayell1
Instagram:	www.instagram.com/ ritamayell\
LinkedIn:	www.linkedin.com/in/ RitaMayell

ENDNOTES

1   Matthew Gordon Lasner, *High Life: Condo Living in the Suburban Century* (New Haven, CT: Yale University Press: 2012), 166.
2   Ibid, 208.
3   Ibid, 104.
4   Ibid.
5   Arthur Pangborn, "Buildings Show City's Growth: Long Beach Structures to Be Run on Co-operative Plan," *Los Angeles Times,* March 25, 1923.
6   "Biggest Liner Here with World Record," *New York Times,* May 17, 1922.
7   "Fact #915: March 7, 2016 Average Historical Annual Gasoline Pump Price, 1929-2015," *Energy.gov,* accessed March 21, 2018, https://energy.gov/eere/vehicles/fact-91 5-march-7-2016-average-historical-annual-gasoline -pump-price-1929-2015.
8   "Cost of Living 1941," *The People History,* accessed March 21, 2018, http://www.thepeoplehistory.com/1941.html.

9   Kirk Myers, "Civil War, Arsenic and Old Lace in Pasadena," *Hometown Pasadena*, April 17, 2016, accessed September 14, 2017, https://hometown-pasadena.com/history/civil-war-arsenic-old-lace-in-pasadena/123069.

10 Ibid.

11 Ibid.

12 Ibid.

13 Ibid.

14 Ibid.

15 Ibid.

16 Lasner, 211.

17 Joan Bubnam, "Pasadena Folk Switch Abodes: Residents of Crown City Forsake Own Homes for Apartment Life," *Los Angeles Times*, October 21, 1954.

CPSIA information can be obtained
at www.ICGtesting.com
Printed in the USA
LVHW03s1932050918
589229LV00017B/1472/P

SEP 1 3 2018